Shhh! Can You Hear Him?

A Reflection of Ways that God Speaks to Us with Confirmations That His Word Is True

Dr. Sandra Hayes, PhD

ISBN 979-8-88832-487-5 (paperback)
ISBN 979-8-88832-488-2 (digital)

Christian Faith Publishing
832 Park Avenue
Meadville, PA 16335
www.christianfaithpublishing.com

Printed in the United States of America

I am biased when it comes to mom. This book is dedicated to the best mom in the world, my humble, loving, and virtuous mother, the late Evelyn Brown Magwood. Her love of Christ and family was undeniable. She taught us the statutes of Christ. Her walks and talks aligned with the teachings of the Lord. Her constant encouragement to keep God first took root in my heart and blossomed. Words cannot describe how much I loved and appreciated my mother.

I also dedicate this book to you. It is my hope that you will be motivated, encouraged, and inspired by the details of how God reveals himself to us. Hopefully, it will compel you with urgency to want to know more about him and diligently seek his face. You will learn that whether you seek him early in life or later in life, God will meet you where you are as long as you have a heart to search after him. Prayerfully, you will gain awareness of God at work in your life. Maybe you will learn to trust the Lord and don't quit when life gets hard because you will gain strength through your struggles.

Come, join me on this journey of life when things that happened were not understood but manifested later on the premise that all things work together for good (Rom. 8:28). If we stop long enough to think, we will see how God's plans for our life come together even though we could not see it at the time. Enjoy the journey and learn the lessons embedded in that struggle/situation/event.

"My sheep hear my voice, and I know them, and they follow me: And I give unto them eternal life: and they shall never perish, neither shall any man pluck them out of my hand" (John 10:27–28).

Contents

Acknowledgment

I want to thank God for pouring into my spirit with unrest until I have written what he said. I am nothing without him. Writing a book is hard work but well worth the work for the reward and joy it brings in knowing something read will touch lives and raise awareness of the truth within.

I am grateful for two main reasons that propelled me to want more, do more, and be more throughout my life—my darling daughter, Quanteer Williams, and most humble son, SSgt. Darius Hayes (AF). My three grandchildren are the love of my life—Fallon, Trevor (TJ), and Brandon Williams. These beautiful, spirited grandchildren encourage my heart to never stop learning. They pour into my hearing new things from this generation that is so different from my generation, and I love it. Thank you, my darling children and adorable grandchildren.

Aunt Rosalie Simmons, our family's matriarch, thank you for your unconditional love, prayers, and support. You are a virtuous woman, and I love you dearly. This book would not have been possible without the encouragement of so many people who saw potential in my writings. Throughout my military career, I would write family and friends and often ended up with laughter because I am a detailed person who would set the atmosphere of the mood from my surroundings while I wrote. My dear friend Annie Bloedorn from DuPont does not hesitate to tell me that she loves to read what I wrote because she can place herself in the scene as if she is there. She makes me laugh.

Thank you to my siblings who made fun of my seven-or-more-pages letters that were referred to as books. This will always be a good laugh, especially because my male siblings would say, "Don't write me, write my wife. She will tell me what you said." I love all of you very much.

Where do I begin? I am eternally grateful for my nurturing and precious sister, Sylvia Kelley (MSGT retired, AF), who is my number 1 cheerleader and my honest and trustworthy best friend who is always there in time of need. She always celebrates and compliments me on my achievements. She is in my Amen corner. Even though she is younger, in a way, she bossed me around from childhood while pushing me to do more and be more. She was always looking for the next best thing she thought *I* could do and not let go until it was done. She weighed my letters to see by weight if it was a read-now or wait-until-later letter. I love you dearly.

I cannot say enough about George Bunch (SGM Army retiree), my male best friend forever (BFF) for now. This God-fearing man is a blessing to behold. George was the most consistent of anyone who never let me forget over the years about my calling to write books. "San, when are you going to start that book?" "San, you need to be writing." He practically willed me to write, although he, too, laughed at my details. "Can you just tell me what happened while leaving out the details of why or how it happened?" He is so funny. Thank you for your encouragement, support, and prayers and for not letting me sit on my gift of writing because others could benefit from what I have to say. He would often say, "You have a message, San, so tell the world what you have to say." I appreciate you so much.

When my mother was diagnosed with Alzheimer's over fifteen years ago, I started an email prayer warriors contact list with my family and military and civilian friends. It started out with "Let me tell you the cute things Mom did" and over time changed into updates of progressive signs of dementia. The prayer warriors would pray with and for my family, and it turned into prayer requests from around the states and overseas. Other prayer warriors whose parent(s) eventually developed Alzheimer's gave thanks to me, letting them know what to expect throughout my mom's experience. Some of these prayer warriors would ask me when am I going to write that book even though I had never mentioned writing before to them. Well, it is here. Thank you for letting me know about your interest in reading my books. The prayers and support that we give to each other and our families cannot be measured.

I asked God to strategically place people in my path to help bring into manifestation those things that he purposed in my heart. When I was finished writing my manuscript, I said, "Lord, I need a publisher." What soon flashed across my television was Christian Faith Publishing (CFP). I had never seen CFP on television before until then, and I have not seen it on television since then. I knew this was for me. From my heart to yours, I am sending a great big cyber hug to everyone at CFP who came in contact with my manuscript. You are awesome! With the very first call from Ms. Marie Lewis, a senior literary agent, my spirit rejoiced. My heart intertwined with that beautiful spirit within that, for me, couldn't be denied. You warmed my heart. In what you said and how you said it, I could feel the presence of the Lord's spirit all over you. That gave me calm and assurance that I was in the right place. Thank you, Ms. Jennifer Brown, publication specialist; you are tenacious. You made contact with me as the publicist and kept me abreast every step of the way. You did not fail to return calls or reach out to me whether I called you or not. I knew you had my best interest at heart. I did not have to wait for an email response or update. It was waiting for me. Thank you. To the editors, I smiled when I saw all those blue marks. I was most pleased that I did not see mostly red marks as in my doctoral program, *phew!* I still wrestle with concise sentences. Everything is important to me, but you shortened my sentences for clarity and understanding. I am amazed at the turnaround time from receipt of my manuscript until the first edit review was sent back to me. Writing a book is hard work, but editing line by line seems harder. I appreciate you and the suggestions you gave to bring clarity where a thought was unclear. You are amazing. Thank you.

Finally, to my gospel community radio hosts at Praise 104.1 FM, I love you. This twenty-four-hour radio station ministers to my heart all day, every day. The only time my radio is turned off from this station is when I am vacationing or going to bed. I have had many praises and worships glorifying God throughout the day. As I continued to write each day and listen to the background music, the songs were constant reminders that God had this under control. Keep writing and keep going forward. Erica Campbell, Willie Moore Jr., Darlene McCoy, Donnie McClurkin, Cheryl Jackson, and the on-air personalities associated, thank you for the uplifting music poured out to the community. They were and are a blessing to me.

Introduction

We all share similar stories and experiences throughout our walks of life, though the outcome may be different. God spoke to many in the Bible through visions, dreams, and confirmations from and through others (prophets/disciples) that which he said would come to pass, and it did. Life, as it is today, is not much different from biblical times in terms of people's visions, dreams, confirmations (from known and unknown people), beliefs, wealth, greed, poverty, homelessness, fear, forgiveness, disobedience/obedience, believers and nonbelievers, deception, adultery, faith, hope, love, hate, etc.; similarities and differences still exist.

This book is written for the novice of readers, believers, nonbelievers, or even those who are searching for something to believe in. People need something to believe in to give them hope, assurance, encouragement, motivation, and inspiration—something to look forward to. Hope is universal; it is when we look for something meaningful, fruitful, and uplifting. We need encouragement to remind us that regardless of how dire our situation looks like, we should look for a flicker of hope, a light at the end of the tunnel that signifies better and brighter days.

Globally, a slow recovery from a pandemic and the deadly coronavirus and its variants has crippled many families over the past three years. Hope sometimes feels like hopelessness. Loss of life exceeded six million over the world. Many businesses, especially small businesses, were hit particularly hard and temporarily closed their doors and/or went out of business; job loss increased. A new normal for work and the education system took on a new life of telework or virtual learning. Families often looked to work or school as a channel for work-home life balance, and that suddenly changed. Some children would get a hot meal from school, and it was probably the only place they could get a hot meal for the day. Families were struggling.

Coupled with this new normal and often with no other way to channel frustration, fear, stress, tension, or the pressures of life, physical, mental, emotional, verbal, and sexual abuse increased. Sadly, suicide rates increased to record highs. Alcohol consumption increased. Many of sound mind are now dealing with mental health issues—depression set in; anxiety, frustration, and other negative emotions became a daily part of families' lives. People were looking for ways to cope, ease the tension, or keep hope alive.

Families often had to choose either to buy food or pay for their badly-needed medicines for their medical issues. Moratoriums to postpone mortgage/rent payments were issued for a period to help keep families from being evicted from their homes/apartments. Foreclosures for many could not be avoided, and families were thrust into homelessness.

Much like the coronavirus that has no respect of persons, natural disasters from fires, flood, or tornadoes leveled or destroyed residents' homes. The number for lives lost increased. People needed something to look forward to—an ounce of hope. Many families are still trying to rebuild their lives, livelihood, homes, or move on without their loved ones. For the heads of household whose demise came unexpectedly from these uncontrollable events in life, those left behind are still trying to survive as best they can.

No matter how trying life gets, we need assurance, encouragement, and motivation to keep going. Sometimes, we have to encourage ourselves. Encouragement often brings back hope and a sense of purpose to not quit at life, to survive. It is too easy to quit; we just stop. As dire as some situations are, there is always a way out; try God. God is the one constant that never changes, and he wants us to call upon him, for he will see us through. In our hurried state of chaos, struggles, doubt, or confusion, we should pause, to be still long enough to talk to God, to listen to his voice as he speaks to us and seek his guidance and direction.

Lessons that are learned from events beyond our control are constant reminders that *if* we stopped long enough to pay attention to the slightest details of what God is saying to us and what he is doing in our lives, we *would* pause long enough to listen. We *would* pause long enough to adhere to his prodding and allow him to direct our paths. This book will show evidence of God at work in every facet of my life, my struggles or situations. Let us go through this journey together, which is evidenced by listening to God's still/sweet voice, thanking him for my obedience and his forgiveness.

This book will reflect how God worked in my life. Once you stop and think about your life, likewise, you may see God at work. You may remember the urging to do or not do a certain thing. You may remember the near accident that should have taken your life, but you are still here. That "something told me" voice that we sometimes dismiss may have been the voice of God that could have changed the trajectory of our lives. Hopefully, this book will raise awareness about our hurried lives and everyday experiences, that if we slow down long enough to see God at work in everything we do, we will get a closer walk with him.

You will see that even when you are going through your valleys, whatever the struggle, look for hope within. Sometimes your valleys may feel more like a storm. Our storms are unique to us, but no one will have your personal experiences as you do. Still, trust God through your storm and learn the lesson while in the storm. May you gain increased faith, strength to stand, and wisdom, knowing God is with you all the way. May you find motivation, encouragement, and inspiration even through your valley of challenges. Know that your valleys (struggles) are for you to go "through" but not to stay there. You are merely passing through to a better you with renewed strength. The testimonies of how I came through my valleys/struggles are evidences of God at work in my life. I declare and decree that I am nothing without him.

My testimonies are not for me; I lived it, and I know the outcome. It is to encourage your hearts that as you go through your challenges, you will realize that trouble don't last always. You will see that nothing can stop the destiny that God has upon your life. God will stop or block anything that tries to hinder where he wants to take you. He will open doors for you that he knows need to be opened and no man can close. He will close doors for you that he knows need to be closed and no man can open. Walk in faith with an "I trust you, Lord" spirit, come what may, and watch how God works mightily in your life. Come, walk with me through this journey of events that, like yours, were sometimes unpleasant, uncomfortable, or shattering; and in the end, hopefully, your latter days, like mine, will be better than your former days.

CHAPTER 1

In the Beginning

> Write the things, which thou hast seen, and the things, which are, and the things, which shall be hereafter.
>
> —Revelation 1:19

Decades ago, Mitch, one of my dearest and lifetime friends, asked if I ever stopped to think of why God allowed *me* to experience those particular events in my life through dreams, visions, and with people. My response was *no*. Until then, the thought did not cross my mind. But his question took root in my heart. Since then, his question was never forgotten and is now usually at the forefront of my thoughts. God has poured into my hearing and spirit, and that is what will be shared with you.

For most of my childhood, as a mama's girl, I hung around Mom. Mama was the love of my life. When Mom was not at work, for the most part, she was mostly at home or church. I wanted to be home with her, sleep with her, go to work with her, and anything; and everything she would allow me to do with "her," I would do it. Although too young to go to work with her, if she could have taken me,

I would surely go just to be with her. From a very young age, Mom told me that I was so different from her other children, though I did not ask in what way. Throughout my formative years, I dreamt dreams that Mom wanted me to share with the church. Mama felt that those dreams meant something. It is my belief that the church leaders were supposed to interpret those dreams. I was too naive or too ignorant about the knowledge of Jesus that though I felt compelled to write them, that was enough. Those dreams were never shared with the church leaders but written in a spiral notebook used as a journal. As a child, I was always a big kid at heart and not serious about most things. When it was time to be serious, I was all in; but fun, laughter, and being a practical joker were most important to me.

Mom, a virtuous woman like no other woman that I know of, was a devout follower of Christ. Through her struggles, and there were many, she did not speak ill of anyone; and if she did, far be it from our hearing. She was faithful to her teachings of God's Words. More importantly, she lived the life that she taught with her daily walk and talk in Christ. Her strength and dependence were totally upon our Lord and Savior, Jesus Christ. She spoke kindly about people, helped others any way she could, cooked, and ironed for others, all with a cheerful heart. My mom was my shero. Her actions and how she reacted to things that were not so nice that she was confronted with was reciprocated with kindness and sincerity. I always said if I could have half of the virtue that Mom had, my life would be touching others' lives positively while leaving my blueprint/footprints in their hearts.

My formative years began to take shape as I was molded from watching Mama and how she handled trials, struggles, situations, hurt, pain, abandonment, strife, infidelity, and lack of anything/everything as a single parent of ten children. Our home was filled with so much love because all we had was each other. I had a wonderful childhood in our four-room house with no running water, with only outhouses, kerosene lamps, scrub boards (for laundry), outside pumps for water, woodstoves—everything we needed, we had. We were poor, but we did not know that. Mom had Jesus. We had Mom—my Queen Bee, and that was enough. Mama did not have much to give, but what she had, she gave, which was all of herself.

Church for me was bittersweet, a love-and-hate relationship. In the early part of my life, I loved going to church because I wanted to know God's Words. In the same token, I hated going to church; not that we had a choice, but we stayed in church too much and much too long. Reflecting on those childhood days, it was clear that God was working within and through me for a time like this. Our pastor used to deliver sermons at Wesley United Methodist Church, but I would leave church feeling no better than what I did when I first got there.

I would look up toward heaven and say, "God, what is he saying?" I tried to follow what the pastor preached, but his delivery had so much theatrics and wailing. Theatrics is what I called the entertainment when delivering a sermon; it was hard to understand God's words that he tried to convey because my focus was on his theatrics and wailing/yelling. This angered me more than anything else, and thereby, it completely turned me off from wanting to go back to church. I wanted to know more of Christ; I just did not know how to get more knowledge of him from what I was introduced to while in church.

Going to church…what does that really mean? To many of us, this means "going to church" physically, of which I imagined God saying, "Forasmuch as this people draw near me with their mouth, and with their lips do honor me, but have removed their heart far from me and their fear toward me is taught by the precept of men" (Isa. 29:13). The thought of my belief was that God can see our mouths say one thing, but our hearts were far removed from him, which, indeed, made me stop long enough to think. Spiritually, going to church was one of the biggest challenges for me. Going to church was brutal because my body was physically there; but I was spiritually, emotionally, and mentally far removed. Our childhood days were filled with Bible study, youth group meetings, Wednesday-night prayer meetings, revivals, and going to services at other churches on Sunday evenings and, sometimes, even on weekdays.

Events were consistently ongoing within churches to raise money. Oftentimes, we had a brown envelope with us to ask people for money to help us with the benevolent fund, baby contest, youth group, and other things; I especially disliked those times. We had to raise money to help the church, but the problem was, all of us had an envelope, and many of us attended the same church or nearby churches, went to the same schools, and were doing the same thing—asking for donations. Those were trying times for me so much so that even now, *if* I ever ask for anything, make no mistake about it, I really need the help.

My childhood days were so much fun. Although we were poor, we were rich in spirit, in heart, and in love for one another. Nowadays, whenever we want a good laugh, my sister Sylvia and I would take walks down memory lane and go back home to our childhood days. Those were the good old days. There was so much laughter, love, joy, and happiness. Having fun, being a kid at heart, and being a practical joker best described my character. I rarely took anything seriously. This was troublesome for my younger sister, Sylvia. For example, when Lauren (my eldest sister's friend) asked how old I was, before I could say anything, Sylvia said rather gruffly, "Sixteen going on twelve. She ain't never gonna grow up!" As a big kid at heart, I relished in my inner being. As a child, Jesus's name rarely came out of my mouth; I did not feel the spirit of the Lord early in my formative years—maybe I did not know how. I was actually ashamed to say the name of Jesus as a child. What I learned was that we had to seek him, and that was harder. How would I know if I had found him?

God knew my longing to want to know more about him was not taking root in my heart. As a child, what was presented to me were through preaching/theatrics; that was not working for me. One thing that was evident was that I talked to God as I talked to anyone else. That statement alone did not register until years later, when I was having a personal relationship with God and did not know it. That was a direct line to God without my knowledge of it being one. While in church, I would look up toward heaven and say, "Lord, I want to know what he is saying, but I cannot understand anything he says." This was disturbing and was met with anger, but as a child, I expressed myself the only way I knew how. Children do not have as many avenues as adults to release pent-up or negative energy. Adults could get in the car, go for a ride, seek counsel from other grown-ups, go to restaurants, movies, etc., to cool down. I began to have a "don't care" attitude toward going to church.

While in the sixth grade, I accidentally became a member of Wesley United Methodist Church. *Accidentally* because when we attended an evening Sunday service at St. John's Baptist Church, I went up to the altar for prayer. When asked if I knew a leader from our church, I pointed to Leader Ford. When I went back to my seat, my cousin told me that I had joined the church. With strong conviction and rather sternly, my reply was "I most certainly did not!" I went up for prayer! Confirmation of that truth came later, but it was not well received in my heart that I did indeed join the church. I was highly upset. What was supposed to be a prayer request has become giving my hand to Christ. This could not happen; I was not ready and did not know how to get out of that predicament.

The next Sunday, with my sister Jan and our friend Deidra, we were officially announced as having given our hands to Christ. Now, we were on a mission to seek God. Where was he and how do we find him?

Wednesday night's prayer meetings were fun for me; that was better than going to church and were not as long. Prayer meetings were more intimate with a small group of people (local church leaders and families). We had praise and worship with hand-clapping, foot-stomping songs on wooden floors; those were some of the best times that lifted my spirit. After praise and worship, we had to get on our knees and pray. I had no idea what to pray for but stayed on my knees longer for no apparent reason. Afterward, Jan would ask me what I was praying for because I was on my knees for so long. Part of that was pretense because after praying for family, what else was there to pray for? There was still a problem: I did not know what I was supposed to be doing.

After we sang, clapped, and worshiped God, those seeking God had to stand in front of everyone and tell our dreams. I tend to believe they (church leaders) knew if we were ready for baptism by our dreams. For me, that was a joke because my dreams, at that time of my life, were far from spiritual. My dreams were of falling into a bottomless pit (very scary) but never hitting the bottom; falling into a very dark chasm (total darkness); or being chased by monsters, dogs, or anything other than dreams that were spiritual that led to God in my life. Those were recurring and frightening dreams. Baptism was on the way, and this would be behind me soon enough. But baptism would not come until we found the Lord. I had no way of knowing when he was found, but it was tied to dreams—that was clear. Seeking God was taking too long.

Additionally, every midnight, Mom would wake Jan and me to go outside to kneel under the big tree to pray and "seek" God. What? "How would we know when we have found him?" was always the question I asked myself. One night, while praying under the tree, I heard a dog's barking getting closer and closer. Jan and I took off running back into the house while slamming the door shut to get away from the dog. Mom would say, "Shut the door! Keep the devil out!" I did not have the heart to tell Mom we were running from the dog; that worked for me, though. I realized I would never get baptized if my dreams did not change.

Nothing about my persona changed while in my elementary school for seeking God. I was still the practical joker who was looking for fun and a good laugh so much that others did not believe I had joined the church. I remember Delia, one of my classmates, said to me, "You joined the church, but you are the biggest devil." I was having too much fun being a kid to care about her remarks. Fun at school would not be taken from me; home was another thing because that was no longer fun while seeking God. I wondered if my sister Jan was held back from baptism because of my foolishness, denial, or even rebellion from accidentally becoming a member of the church. Jan was not fun to be around, but we were seeking God together. It is my belief that Jan and Deidra were guilty by association because we joined the church at the same time and should be baptized at the same time. I do not know what their dreams were, but mine were not getting me closer to Jesus; I honestly believed I held them up from baptism because of "my" dreams.

There had to be a new strategy for baptism because I was very tired of not doing things that I enjoyed that were fun such as being able to chew gum, eat candy, drink sodas, play cards, have friends come over, or go outside to play. All of that and more were taken away while we sought God. I definitely was tired of going outside at night to seek God. There were so many rules, and I did not like any of them. Something had to be done, so I started making up believable dreams. I spoke of those things I thought they wanted to hear so I could get baptized and stop this foolishness. The strategy in the dreams I told them about sure made a difference. I hated those six months—yes, six long months of seeking and trying to find God. Maybe they had mercy on us and just let us get baptized. I do not know, but God was not closer to me in *heart* even after baptism. I was a work in progress.

June 15, 1969, was that glorious day of baptism—oh, happy day! I wrote that date down as a day to remember because in my thought process, baptism was well earned. Little did I know, God was working on me even then, and I was growing more and more into his will in spite of my ignorance about seeking him. Going to church was still not satisfying for me; I did not like going to church and kept my pocket change to get some candy. In reflection of my formative years, the realization was that God was using me in my innocence while shaping, making, and molding me to be about his business. I developed a relationship with God and had no knowledge that I was getting a closer walk with "him."

For example, at the age of twelve, we had to go to Bethel Baptist Church's evening service. The choir members were those in our community. They did what people called "catching the Holy Ghost." Remember, I am talking about my innocence as a twelve-year-old child while having open communication with God from how *I* saw things. Some choir members were hopping, hollering, crying, and the likes. Do not get me wrong; I realize now that I was a babe in Christ or not even walking in Christ but just recently baptized. Baptism is symbolic of a person dying to sin and living for Christ, and to me, just being baptized does not merely refer to living for Christ. We have to embrace our new Christian walk, but I was not receptive to doing that at the time. Our daily walk and talk should be pleasing unto him. Mine was still in question. Still, there was much to learn with my walk in Christ. That would come later in life.

While looking at the choir members falling all over the place, crying, hollering, and yelling, I looked up toward heaven and said, "Lord, these ain't nothing but a bunch of hypocrites. I see what they do in church, and I see what they do out of church." Wait a minute; this is coming from the heart of a child who has yet to experience life's ups and downs or even find Christ in her heart and soul. My beliefs were what they were *my* beliefs. Choir members were a little older than me. They made it seem like catching the Holy Ghost was the thing to do, not thinking that they could have had some serious issues in life. Anyhow, God must have convicted my heart because it made me pause long enough to address what I said; I looked up once again toward heaven and said with conviction, "Oh no, Lord. I am not a hypocrite! I came to church because Mama made me come. If I had a choice, I would not be here. That does not make me a hypocrite! I had no choice!" God has got to be a humorous god. That was probably the first *revela-*

tion that I can remember of truly talking to God from my heart. Maybe God was at the door of my heart; I just had to let him in. There would be many more conversations with God.

My focus began to change somewhat to showing more gratitude about everything by giving some thought of the situation at hand. The larger things in life did not seem to matter to me. What was important to me was finding ways to help Mom through her struggles as a single parent with so many children. Dad just walked away when I was about six years old and did not look back until I was about to graduate from high school; Mom never abandoned us. She gave us all that she had—love beyond measure. She gave us all of "her"; who could ask for anything more? She was strong, determined, and sought a better life for herself and for us. She never took her eyes off the prize: God; she diligently sought his will and his ways. She was the strongest woman I knew.

December came around fast, and somehow, Mom's facial expressions were etched in my mind. Children ask for toys at Christmas. Mom, as a single parent of ten, was not able to give us a lavish Christmas, if she could give us anything at all. The closer it got to Christmas, the more concerned Mom looked. Her concerned facial expression was a little puzzling to me. The only thing at that time I could associate with her worry was the Christmas gifts for her children. I said, "Mama, if you can't get me anything for Christmas, don't worry about me. Go ahead and get something for the other children. I don't think you will love me any less if you couldn't get me anything for Christmas. I'll be all right."

Little did I know, that had a huge impact for my mom, but that was in my heart, so I told her. Decades later, while on military leave, I visited my mom. Mom asked me if I remembered when I said as a child that she didn't have to get me anything for Christmas. I said, "Yes, Mom, I remember. I must have been a silly child." Mom laughed. As a single parent later in life, I could only have imagined what Mom must have felt like having a child that tried to understand her struggles. That leaves much to admire and appreciate.

I wanted to be just like my older sister. She was so very beautiful with white teeth and a pretty smile. I wanted to follow her everywhere she went, but she would not let me go anywhere with her. Still, my chase was after my sister; she was my idol. One day, I was almost fourteen years old that I had a revelation after seeing a very ugly side of her that hurt me to my heart. I wish I could recount the specifics, but it was something that was directed at someone else in a very ugly and disrespectful tone. That disturbed me greatly; I looked up toward heaven and said, "Lord, I can't be like her. She is so beautiful on the outside but ugly on the inside. I can't be like her." God showed me what he needed me to see. God was shaping, making, and molding me into who he wanted me to be. While still in my formative years, I did not know what I wanted to be, but I knew what I did not want to be, and that was having an ugly spirit that hurt people.

CHAPTER 2

Because of My Ashes

All things work together for good.
—Romans 8:28

Over the decades, I have sifted through my "ashes," good and bad; all were instrumental in becoming the person that I am today. My ashes were the roads that I trod, the ups and downs, life's trials, events that were beyond my control—divorce, overcoming a lack of self-esteem, dignity shot to hell, being stripped of my pride, mental/physical/emotional abuse, etc.—ashes. Having grown up in a four-room house, *not* bedrooms but *four-room* house, with our virtuous mother and nine siblings, ten if you count our first cousin who grew up in our house from adolescence when their house burned down, we took care of each other. All we had were each other and a whole lot of love. My story is not unlike other people's stories, but we got through it—some were unscathed, and some scarred with lasting reminders. For me, my childhood was the good ole days.

In our four-room house, there was no running water; we had a woodstove, a pail for overnight excrements, an outhouse, a pump to get well water—just to give you a visual. We had scrub boards and big tubs to wash and rinse our clothes in (and big tubs to bathe); oftentimes, we bathed in the same water. Winters were brutal on our fingers from washing the clothes and going outside in the cold to hang the clothes on the line, among other things. We had kerosene lamps for light; we eventually got electricity, but that was a long time coming. We hitchhiked everywhere we went as we did not own a car. Mom made almost everything we wore or were hand-me-downs from an older sibling; new clothes were bought only for Easter. Mom did the best that she could, and I appreciated her very much.

We wore the same pair of shoes until the bottom wore out, and then we would put cardboards in our shoes as cushions so the bottom of our feet would not touch the ground, shoes that were passed down from an older sibling and were too large the toes were stuffed with brown paper bags or newspapers—whatever we could put in it for a better fit. Some of you know what I am talking about.

Within our home, my mother had a bedroom while my oldest brother, oldest sister, and three younger brothers shared two bunk-bed sets in the other bedroom. My other two sisters, a cousin, and I slept on a hideaway couch in the living room (LR)—two slept at the head and two at the feet of the couch. When I graduated from HS in 1975, we still had an outhouse, a woodstove, tubs for bathing and washing clothes, and a hideaway bed in the LR. We already had electricity by that time.

During the summertime in our early teenage years, we worked in the fields. A big bus would pick us up by 6:00

a.m. and would bring us back somewhere around 6:30 p.m. every day all day during the summer months except Sundays. We would often work in triple-digit heat; the heat was brutal. We knew nothing about sunscreen lotion, and child labor laws were not enforced, at least, in that part of South Carolina. The ride to the field seemed very long probably because we did not know where we were going. Tomatoes and string beans were the most picked during my adolescent/teenage years. We picked tomatoes for $0.25 a bucket or a bushel of string beans for $1 a bushel. We did not know which field we were going to until we got there.

Once we arrived to the field, the driver would drop some of us on one end of the field and drive to the other end of the field for another drop-off. The rows were so very long that we started on each end of the row and met in the middle. Once we finished with that field, they would take us to another field. There was a makeshift dirt road in the field. Long, wooden boxes were stacked along this dirt road as easy access for trucks to drop off loads of empty boxes and pick up filled boxes before and after picking the products. We were given big buckets with a handle so they can be easily picked up and kept moving forward to get to each bush to pick the products. Once we filled our buckets, we lugged those heavy ones on our shoulders for balance, walked across rows to get to the boxes, emptied our buckets of products into the boxes, and received a ticket. Our hands were stained and crusted with green from the tomato bush, which did not easily wash off. That did not matter because the next day, we were back in the field with our stained and crusted hands doing it all over again.

String beans, to me, were the hardest to pick. We had to pick lots of string beans to fill the bushel. I kept a large apron when picking string beans because once half full, the bushels were too heavy to pick up and move along the row. I would hold my apron out, fill it with string beans, and walk back to the bushel to put the string beans in them. Once the sun came out, the heat wilted the string beans, which made them not as firm. When the people who gave us the tickets came to check our bushel to see if they were filled before putting a lid on it, that apron came in handy. They would often push the beans down and then tell us we that need to put some more beans in the bushel before we could get our ticket. I would fill my apron once again with the string beans and put more in the bushel. They would put a lid on the bushel, lock it down, and give me a ticket. Those were back-breaking days of which I do not ever want to experience again.

They gave us tickets much like those that were given at a door prize at an office function for each bucket or bushel we picked. We kept those tickets in our pockets and made sure we did not lose them because at the end of the day, we stood in long lines to cash in our tickets to get paid. We knew not if we were cheated because they paid us in cash and told us to keep the line moving. Very recently, George, a very dear and forever friend, hearing about our adolescent/teenage work life, said that this sounded like we were migrant workers. The thought never crossed my mind until then; as I looked back and reflected, I would say yes, indeed. That sounds like we were migrant workers, but we didn't know what we didn't know.

Several years ago, I had the pleasure of touring the African American Museum in DC with my girlfriend Diva. As we toured the ground floor, I walked slowly in front of her, taking in the worst time in the African American history. Diva, who is from Michigan, called my name; and I went back to see what she wanted. She smiled, pointed, and said, "Look, Sandra." She pointed at a scrub board for washing clothes because she had not seen one in real life.

Without a thought, I said, "Yeah, I know. I grew up using that," and I kept walking. Realizing she was not behind me, I went back to see what was wrong. She froze and looked listless with a blank stare. She wouldn't move; she stood there, motionless. I asked her what was wrong. With teary eyes and a cracking voice, she said, "I am feeling some kind of way."

"Why?" I asked.

"Because," she said, "you are not that much older than me. I have heard of people using a scrub board and wash tub, but I don't know anyone *personally* who used one." She struggled to fight back tears, and then she shut down; she did not want to talk about what she saw, and we never spoke of that again because she can't process the possibility of "*knowing*" someone around her same age group living under those conditions. She said this was difficult for her to process. To this day, she avoids any topic about that awakening in her life.

My past is just that—my past. I do not look back at my past with contempt, and if I do look back, I use it as a stepping stone to a better future. I am the person that I am today because of my ashes, coupled with surviving a mental/emotional/verbal/physical abuse (once) and infidelity from a prior marriage as part of my ashes to make me "more." After my dignity, pride, and self-esteem were stripped from that marriage, I had to shift my focus. With no thought of the realization in front of me, I had become a product of my environment by projecting, through what I said and did, those hurtful words that were fed into my ears throughout my short marriage. "The women in SC are illiterates," he would say.

"But, baby, you married a woman from SC."

"Oh," he said, "you are a 'functional' illiterate."

Those were dark days and not one I like to revisit. I had allowed his knowledge to intimidate me, so I fought my way back. With what was said and done in my marriage, that propelled me forward and helped to pave my path for a better future. The fight was against those horrible things that I allowed to be fed into my spirit: "You are dumb, stupid, and a functional illiterate." My inner self screamed, "No!" Those negative things that were used to describe or label me were not true. I am not dumb; I am not stupid. I can, I can, I can! We do not have to stay in the state of affairs/mindset of our struggles or beliefs. We are stronger than what we believe. My belief in my "more" gave me strength to continue the fight for more livelihood, more laughter, more self-esteem, more dignity, more zest, more zeal, more pride, more of "me" and what I can do to make my life and my children's lives better! The hunger for "more" was greater than the ashes of depression or any other negative charges within; I wanted *more* positive things that life had to offer—more happiness, more joy, more peace. I wanted *more* of everything good and fewer tears!

While crying out to Maria, my babysitter, "Maria, I am tired of crying. I don't want to cry anymore."

She would say, "No, Sandra, you are not tired of crying."

Other times, I would cry yet again, "I am tired of crying, Maria. I am sick and tired of crying."

Have you ever felt like that? Maria must have heard me say that one time too many, but in her calm, sweet, angelic voice, she would say, "No, Sandra, you are not tired of crying."

Puzzled from her response, my tone shifted to a more stern approach. "Why do you keep saying I am not tired of crying, Maria? I am tired of crying. I don't want to cry anymore!"

She said, "Sandra, when you get sick and tired of being sick and tired, you gonna do something about it."

The "how" she said resonated in my spirit more than the "what" she said; this was not forgotten, and she was right. That was my wake-up call.

One day, I looked up to heaven and said, "Lord, I don't know what I am going to do. I got a newborn baby and a school-aged child. I'll go through whatever I have to go through, Lord, but he has to go." I told my then husband that he had to go and that he could leave escorted or unescorted, but leave he will; he left. It was then that I stepped out on faith; the marriage was over. I went through some things but gained so much strength along the way. My tears nowadays shifted from those of sadness to joy.

Before the divorce, with a newborn baby and a school-aged child, in seeking better and wanting "more," my enlistment into the Army was a welcomed change. I was fast-tracked in the Army for promotions because I refuse to believe that I could not be or do something. I was promoted to Staff Sergeant (SSG) within four years and ten months of service. My promotion in the senior-enlisted rank to Sergeant First Class (SFC) was achieved well ahead of my peers (about nine years of service). With eleven years into the military, I was accepted into the Warrant Officer Corps. I earned my Master's Degree in Human Resource Management as a Warrant Officer 1 (WO1) and retired as a Chief Warrant Officer 3 (CW3) after twenty-one years of military service.

Let's not get this twisted. Early on in my military career was a daily struggle. Many times, I chastised myself for not knowing how to do a task that was seemingly easy for my peers but not for me. My struggle was to believe in my abilities of learning, knowing, and doing with efficiency any task at hand and to release those ugly words that held me captive for so long; I believed I was *not* dumb, stupid, or a functional illiterate. Doubt sometimes tried to creep in my thoughts, but I worked hard to block doubt and uncertainty out; I fought back, and I won.

My struggle, though, was not in vain. I did not do the tasks that were seemingly easy to do efficiently, but my refusal not to quit learning was stronger. It is too easy to quit; we just stop doing whatever our task/challenge is when we quit. My thoughts about my lack of abilities were those of bondage, therefore projecting negative beliefs in my actions and in my deeds. My struggles lessened, and I learned how to do more of any task. My confidence in myself grew, and rarely was there a reminder of my ineptness to learn. The reinforcement of my new beliefs began to take a form in itself. That was refreshing, for I was learning more and more.

After my retirement from the Army in September 2005, my prayer was that God would bless me with a job that allows me to make lots of money and has no stress—granted. I was hired as a contractor in November 2005 and subsequently a year later as a Senior Management Analyst of the Department of the Army Civilian (DAC) until retirement in January 2019. My quest for knowledge kept emerging. Throughout my tenure as a DAC, I earned my PhD from Capella University in 2016 and became an adjunct professor at Webster University shortly thereafter. My resignation from Webster University in May 2020 was well deserved. I have arrived! Throughout the decades, I worked hard and toiled long. Now, it is time to reap the benefits of my labor. With pleasure, I bask in the new chapter of my life—retirement.

People often associate my work life with my military and federal service, but they do not see or know about my "ashes"—those back-breaking work from my years in the sun in triple-digit heat throughout the summer months of my youth, coupled with work after HS graduation and into the military. People often do not remember those things that were before our ashes, but they will only remember those things that are beyond our ashes. "Dr. Sandra Hayes"—that is what is remembered, not my ashes. They do not know that it was my "ashes" that propelled me forward to become Dr. Sandra Hayes.

My choice was not to sift through my ashes but to allow myself to bask in the feelings of euphoria and total peace for not having to "stay" in that potentially crippling state of mind/affairs. The ashes of my past were a rite of passage for me to walk into an endless world of possibilities in the hopes of living my best life ever. My past was used as a stepping stone to a better future and moving forward with dreams that far exceeded anything imaginable to me at the time. When I think of where I was and how far I have come, my spirit rejoices! My peace of mind is paramount and priceless. The tranquility brought by my peace of mind is nonnegotiable, for I know what it is like to be on the opposite side of the spectrum without any. No one is allowed to take my peace, for I hold it steadfastly simply because it belongs to me.

I make no excuses for not being strong enough to fight during those dark days of my life, for my strength came from the fights of life. I have gained a great sense of appreciation because of my past, and I am stronger because of my ashes. My ashes were described as the struggle of growing up with much of nothing and working my way upward. That is my story—history/his-story/her-story does not have to be your story. Write your own script, your own story! There was nothing easy about fighting my way through obstacles, but choosing to stand and fight made me victorious. "My latter days are far greater than my former days" (Job 8:7).

While assigned to HHC, VII Corps in Stuttgart, Germany, in the mid-1980s, Paul Harvey, an Armed Forces

Network (AFN) radio commentator often closed his segment with a profound statement: "Give me a fish, I'll eat for today. Teach me to fish I'll eat every day." That resonated in my spirit and became my mantra throughout the decades. With those words etched in my mind, it was easy to go fishing daily. That renowned phrase taught me how to get my own fish (money, resources, necessities of life, etc.). My reliance was totally on God and not merely on man to show me how and where to fish.

A return on investment (ROI) is a term commonly used in business. I used that as a basis to encourage myself and others to return from ashes (RFA)—those things that were or are not pleasant in our lives, the struggles and asking ourselves, "Why is there so much month left at the end of the money? How am I going to pay for my child's education?" You know, those ashes, those struggles that weigh a person down or being stuck between a rock and a hard place, so to speak. Try to go fishing through your mounds of ashes into everything good that life has to offer. Go fishing and don't quit!

CHAPTER 3

God Speaks to Us through Visions and Dreams

August 1981

This era of my life can probably be pronounced as the beginning of my knowledge in my walk for Christ. My walk and talk were different. My growth and development in my walk with God became more evident. My dreams were starting to be spiritual and began to have meaning in my life.

I dreamt that I was alone and playing in an open field. Appearing out of nowhere, there was a little white lamb and a human. The little white lamb was walking in an upright position on its two hind legs. The little white lamb's left paw was in the human's right hand. They started walking slowly away from me.

They walked a short distance from me, hand in hand, and they stopped. The human never turned around; all I saw was the back of him, but the little white lamb turned around and pointed at me. His voice thundered as he pointed at me, saying, "The Lord said, 'When I call, you will come!'" I began to cry, and my mom came and asked what was wrong. I said, "When the Lord comes, I would die."

She said, "The Lord said he would be back again."

Dreams can tell us important things about ourselves—things we need to know or even things to come. God knows our heart and wants a heart that desires to search after him. Maybe God was calling me more into his service. I had to get more into his will to be about his business. I believed he showed me his glory because we know that no one has seen God's face and lived (Exod. 33:20), but the message was clear of his calling. Jesus is the Lamb of God and the light of the world. Please, Lord, show me what to do and how to do it.

Moses

May 1986 dream
1st Infantry Division, Ft. Riley, Kansas

God is continually working in us and through us. When God has a message for us or a message to someone else through us, we do not know "how" he will come to us.

In this dream, I was at home in our blue house in South Carolina. My best friend from high school, Carlene, and others were there. We were having fun and preparing breakfast. There was a knock on the door, and I answered it. A man was standing there, asking for directions to go somewhere (I can't remember the place). I told him how to get there, and he left.

Later that day, while driving my blue Chevette, I looked in the rearview mirror and saw a large snake. I said to myself, *I'd better stop this car and get that snake before it crawls under the seat and bites me.* I pulled my Chevette to the curb and pulled up the hatch. A man dressed in white was in the trunk. I told him to be careful; that there is a snake in the car, and it might bite him. The man got out of the trunk, stood up, and said in a reassuring voice, "He won't bite you."

He had a rod in his hand; the snake curled around the loop of the rod and went on about its business. He said, "My name is Moses, and I want to thank you."

I asked, "Thank me for what?"

He said, "For telling me how to get to ____________" (wherever that place was when he knocked on our door asking for directions). I looked at him, puzzled, and said, "But that wasn't you," while referring to the person who came to our door earlier that morning.

He said in a calm and soothing voice, "Oh, but it was very much me."

We do not know how God will reveal himself to us. We can often bear witness of people who may have crossed our paths who we did not assist in some way. Thank God for the sweet reminders of who he is in our lives and what he would have us to do. In Matthew 25:35–40, God spoke of us inheriting the kingdom that was prepared for us because he was hungry and was fed; thirsty and was given drink; a stranger and was taken in; naked and was clothed; sick and was visited; in prison, and we came to him. Inasmuch as was done to the least of these brethren, it was done unto him. When we usher in his presence, we strive to let our daily walk and talk be pleasing unto him. Furthermore, we should be careful how we treat people because we could be entertaining angels unawares. The man who came to our door might have been an angel.

Heaven-bound

HHC, VII Corps Stuttgart, Germany, 1988

Sometimes, we are so bombarded with life's trials, strife/contentions, ups and downs, marriages/divorces, struggles, etc., that stare us in the face. Those events may take us out of the element of peace that God wants us to have. God's word said in John 14:27, "Peace I leave with you, my peace I give unto you: not as the world giveth, give I unto you. Let not your heart be troubled, neither let it be afraid."

Sometimes, we get so caught up in life and its challenges that it disturbs our peace with God. When this happens, we may not focus on God's peace because we address the issues at hand that may be many. We may not have the time to stop and feel the peace of God with so much to do, and we miss him (God) and his presence. When we keep God first in our heart, thoughts, and mind, regardless of what we go through, we will feel the presence, peace, and joy that only he can give.

My dream: I was in my apartment when my ex-husband appeared. In my hand was a medallion with a cross in the middle. He was trying to take the medallion with the cross from me, and I kept saying, "No, you can't have it," as I held it in a closed fist against my heart with my other hand over it for protection. Angrily, he chased me around the room, determined to take it from me as he said firmly, "Give it to me!"

I clenched the medallion with the cross tightly in my hand and held it closer to my heart. I kept saying, "I can't let you have it! I can't let you have it."

By this time, he had cornered me, and there was nowhere to run—no escape. He said angrily again, "Give it to me!"

I yelled, "No, I won't give it to you!"

As I tried to hold fast to the medallion with the cross while being cornered, I was lifted up from the floor. I felt as light as a feather as I floated from the floor through the ceiling, through the stars, and through the night. When I stopped from being lifted upward toward heaven, it was daylight and I found myself sitting upon clouds while looking in amazement. There were many people just looking at me with smiles and glee in their eyes. No one spoke a word; they were just looking at me and smiling. It felt so good, and I felt safe.

With our natural eyes, we may not see a way out, but God can make a way of escape from our perils of life, adversity, troubles, or stumbling blocks in our paths. Numbers 6:25–26 says, "The Lord make his face shine upon thee, and be gracious unto thee; The Lord lift up his countenance upon thee, and give thee peace." We should search diligently for God's peace, for he desires that we feel more of him and less of life's chills.

Stuttgart, Germany, 1989

"Choose ye this day whom you will serve" (Josh. 24:15).

When we choose to seek validation from others, we lose sight of the road we are to tread in the name of the Lord for "his" validation. We may become crowd pleasers to be accepted and included. God may have a different road for us to tread, but we have to be mindful of him and careful not to be fooled merely by the pleasures of life.

In this dream, there was a large crowd of people in the middle of a large opening, as in a field, surrounded by trees/forest. There was a playground nearby but void of children. There was so much chaos and confusion among the people. All of a sudden, the people started scurrying, running away. They ran fast, and I tried to run just as fast to catch them. I kept saying, "I can't let them leave me," but I could not catch up to them; they were too fast.

My attempts to run harder to catch them were to no avail. The distance between them and me grew further apart. I knew I had to catch them, or they would leave me. Suddenly, the palm of a very large hand appeared in front of my face, which stopped me, and with a loud and stern voice, I heard, "NO! You go that way." The index finger on the hand pointed in the direction behind me to a narrow path in the opposite direction. I turned back around and thought, "It's just a narrow path" as I headed in that direction—alone.

Sometimes we have to pull away from people, places, and things to grow in Christ. I tried to keep up with the crowd but could not; that was not in God's plans for me. "For I know the thoughts that I think toward you, saith the Lord, thoughts of peace, and not of evil, to give you an expected end" (Jer. 29:11). I do not know what the end plans the Lord has for me, but those plans were not in following others. I chose to follow and serve God, not man.

The road that is prepared for us to travel may seem like we are alone. If we keep our heart and mind on Jesus, we know we are not alone. When we pay attention to his words, we will know that he said, "Straight is the gate, and narrow is the way, which leadeth unto life, and few there be that find it" (Matt. 7:14). Let us keep as a purpose in our hearts to be one of the few that are wise enough to find the straight and narrow way that leads to Christ.

Warrant Officer Candidate School (WOCS)

Fort Rucker, Alabama
November 1995

Becoming a Warrant Officer (WO) was not on my radar as a goal while in the Army. My heart was set to become a Drill Sergeant (DS) or a First Sergeant (1SG). I wanted to shape and mold young and impressionable minds, giving them a firm foundation and a sense of purpose before they got totally integrated in the Army. The opportunity for either DS or 1SG did not present itself; those were not God's plans for me. Little did I know, over a decade later, because of a serious medical diagnosis, I probably would not have survived the all-day strenuous activities associated with the demands of being a DS or 1SG. "All things work together for good" (Rom. 8:28). I see the good more and more in my life as I learned to trust God even through the ups and downs of my life.

When my forever sister/friend, Nessa, badgered me to go to Warrant Officer Candidate School (WOCS) under the buddy system, I emphatically said no; I wanted to be a DS/1SG, *not* a warrant officer. After much badgering, I relented and gave in because I knew, without a shadow of a doubt, my application would not be selected for WOCS due to lack of experience. My belief was strong because, at that time, my experience in multifunctional personnel management/services was minimal. My initial enlistment contract was as an Administrative Specialist (71L) of which I worked for five years. Later, my request to reclass/retrain from an Administrative Specialist to Personnel Management Specialist as a Staff Sergeant (SSG) was approved; therefore, acceptance into the WOCS was hard to believe because I did not have years of experience in personnel management, which was often a requirement in that field. I must say, after the badgering, Nessa still did not submit her warrant officer packet, and I went alone—shame on her (LOL). I believe that becoming a WO was part of God's plans for me, but he used Nessa as the vessel to get me there. Amen!

I was accepted with my first submission to WOCS. The WOCS prepared us to be technicians in our field of study from a baseline of our previous Military Occupational Skill (MOS), of which I had limited experience. Coupled with my lack of personnel management experience, the WOCS was the hardest military school to get accepted into and not governed under the regulations of the Army's Training and Doctrine Command (TRADOC) at the time. Soldiers in my office at Fort Meade took dibs that I would be back within two weeks because that was the norm for those sent back to their home station before completion of WOCS training. There was no oversight on the warrant officer school at that time. I was told of complaints of injustices and discrimination that were raised, and an investigation ensued. One of my dearest sister-friends filed a complaint as she was sent back from WOCS before completion of training for one reason or another. It seems that the investigation found the allegations to be true—that 33 percent is the attrition rate of blacks, particularly black females; they were sent back before completion of WOCS training. Drastic changes were then made. Our warrant officer class was the first to go through the WOC training under TRADOC's oversight.

Training as a WOC was rigorous, tiring, exhaustive, challenging, and stressful. It was not uncommon for multiple commands to be thrown at us simultaneously—to have high-speed building/room changes in the wee hours of the morning while being screamed at to hurry up, hang up our uniforms, put our clothes in the drawers, make up the bed, and then get in bed. This was a test of the mind, will, tenacity, and to show that we paid attention to details.

One night, while in WOCS training, I had a dream that I was standing on the shore of a beach, soaking in the sun and admiring the view of the water that seemed to have no end. Out of nowhere, I saw a huge wave forming afar and told myself, "I had better get off this beach before that big wave hits me."

No sooner than I said that, the huge wave overshadowed and engulfed me in a circular motion, as if scooping me up from where I stood on the shore. I could see my body swirling around within it helplessly. Suddenly, a large hand reached in the wave, grabbed me by the back of my collar, lifted me out of that dangerous wave, and placed me farther back on the shore. God is full of "suddenlies."

Later that evening, after training, I told my roommate about the dream, and she chuckled and asked, "Don't you know what just happened?" I said, "No, I don't know what the dream meant."

She said, "The enemy will come in like a flood but the Spirit of the Lord shall lift up a standard against it" (Isa. 59:19). Nothing can stop the destiny that God has for me. It seems God was telling me that all would be well. God was with me all the way, and he still is with me every step of the way.

Prepared for the Kingdom

Personnel Service Support Team (PSST),
MacDill AFB, Florida, 1998

"All things work together for good" (Rom. 8:28).

God knows what he is doing; I trust him. We may ask why things happen to us and not stop to think that they may all be a part of God's plan. If we pay attention to the slightest details of our lives, we will see God at work, preparing us all along the way to get through our struggles and be ready for eternal life.

In my dream, three of my sisters and I were in South Carolina headed to the airport. For some reason, we had to go back to our house. Sylvie and James were in the car, and the others felt that we took too long, so they decided to meet us at the airport.

I ran in our house to tell Mom we were leaving. Auntie was standing in the hallway with her back against the wall. She had some tears trickling down her face. I looked at her and said, "Look at you standing there, looking like Grandmama. Dry up those tears." We smiled, and I went further into the house. There stood Grandmama, who died years earlier. I smiled as I said to her, "Grandmama, I love you." She smiled but never said a word. I went into the bedroom where Mom and Dad were (Dad died in 1985) to tell them we were leaving for the airport.

Mom was lying on her right side, not acknowledging me in the room, and Dad was standing at the foot of the bed. I looked at him and said, "Give me a kiss before I go." As I moved toward him, he held up his hand to motion me to stop as he said, "No, you can't touch me!" Dad had a circle of light glowing all around him as he said that. It looked like a light that surrounded the depiction of Jesus on his ascension to heaven. There was a stillness, some peace and calm in the room. I left the room at that point to go to the airport.

Sylvia and I started running to get to the highway behind the house where Auntie Gal used to live. What was once an old, dilapidated house was now a mansion with a marbled gate, marbled sidewalk, and everything surrounding the mansion were marbled. We opened the gate and began to run across the huge yard as a shortcut to get to the highway. The mansion was beautiful. A tiny little puppy started to follow us; I knew Sylvia was afraid of dogs, so I turned around, pointed, and yelled to the puppy, "Go back. You can't go with us! The puppy looked sad as it turned away and went back. We kept running, and again, there was the puppy, trying to catch up with us. I told him once again to go back and threw a newspaper at him to scare him off so he wouldn't follow.

When I turned around, Sylvia was nowhere in sight; she had already reached the highway, but there were so many people, I could not find her. I called out her name, "Sylvia!"

I heard the Spirit of the Lord say, "She's over there" as I saw a finger pointing to the direction on my left.

Then the Spirit of the Lord said, "I'm just trying to prepare you, my sweet, to meet the king!" There was a parting through the crowd of people, and a path was made between the people where they were on opposite sides of each other. As the path cleared, I could see Sylvia sitting on a large, beautiful, marble throne. Jesus said in John 14:2–3, "In my Father's house are many mansions: if it were not so, I would have told you. I go to prepare a place for you. And if I go and prepare a place for you, I will come again, and receive you unto myself; that where I am, there ye may be also."

I love the thought of God preparing me for his kingdom for that great day when I cease to exist on earth. It is my desire to hear my God say, "Well done, thou good and faithful servant. Enter into the kingdom."

The Name of Jesus

F Detachment, 18th Personnel Services Battalion (PSB)
Fort Polk, LA
February 10, 2001

God's words say in Philippians 2:10–11, "At the name of Jesus, every knee should bow, of things in heaven, and things in earth, and things under the earth; and that every tongue should confess that Jesus Christ is Lord, to the glory of God the Father." Jesus is the sweetest name I know. Jesus's name comes out of my mouth every day of the week, regardless if things were good or not so good, for I know Jesus is in the midst of everything I do.

In my dream, we were riding in a car, and a darling little girl sat on my lap. The little girl said in an angelic voice, "I just want a coat." She seemed a bit sad. Later, I found myself in a clothing store, holding three little girl's coats, trying to decide which of the three coats would be purchased. Then, a couple (a man and a woman) approached me. It seemed like they were my friends; they had a familiar spirit, I suppose. I told them I wanted to buy a coat for the little girl. The lady said, "Don't worry about that," and she took the coats from me and laid them on a rack.

We walked out of the store. She was telling me about a man whom she thought liked me but had two little girls at home. I told her I didn't think he was interested in me;

I think he liked one of my other friends. As we kept walking, the lady was to my left side, and the man was to my right; but no one said anything else while we walked. As we walked farther, we were approaching a large overhead arch. Before we walked through the arch, the man veered off to the far right, and only the woman and I walked through the arch.

The arch looked like a pathway, but flowers grew over and around its frame. I looked around as we walked through the flowered arch and wondered why snakeheads were bobbing through the flowers, and more importantly, I wondered why she bought me here. I kept looking around at the snakeheads bobbing through the flowers around the arch as we continued through the long arch. The female did not seem to take notice or cared; she looked straight ahead and kept walking. Neither of us said anything. I had no idea where we were going, but I kept walking with her.

We exited the arch and entered into a large clearing (a desertlike scene) that had a big hole, as in a burial ground of snakes, as soon as we exited the arch. There was a large cobra-head snake monument in front of the large hole. We walked further; there was another large hole/pit, much like another burial ground for snakes. The woman never said a word. As we kept walking deeper into this desertlike place, seeing more of the same, I stopped, and so did she. However, she did not change her position; her body and eyes stayed in the same direction of her walk—straight ahead. I looked at her and said, "We have to go back." She just stood there, and it felt like this was a setup. I told her

I would not take another step, that we must go back. She did not move.

I started to run back in the only direction that I knew, which was the way we came in through the arch, and she also started running. Shortly thereafter, her footsteps stopped behind me, and I turned around to see why. I could see she was not going back because she just stood there. I turned back around and started running again toward the arch. Ahead, I could see people coming out of the ground with shovels, hoes, tools, etc., as they formed a barrage to block my path so I could not get out. I saw no one other than the woman walking with me when we came through that arch; now, people were coming from everywhere out of the ground to form a barrage to keep me in there. They blocked the exit from afar, but I kept running toward the exit, yelling in a very loud voice, "In the name of Jesus, let me pass! In the name of Jesus, let me pass!" Immediately, they moved out of my way with outstretched arms, one hand touching the other. This felt like the parting of the Red Sea where they formed a path to each side of the arch. I kept running, demanding, "In the name of Jesus, let me pass! Hallelujah! Glory, Jesus!" The more I called on Jesus's name, the more they kept making a clear path while moving out of my way. I exited that desert with no problems, for God cleared the path for me. Thank you, Lord!

The enemy tried to stop me, but Jesus came and blocked them. The name of Jesus was as a ram in the bush and a way of my escape from harm. Scripture reminds us to submit yourselves, therefore, to God. "Resist the devil, and he will flee from you" (James 4:7). No one or nothing can stop God's plans for my life.

Trumpets and Chariots

Fort Polk, LA
February 2002

Niecey is my dear friend and sister at heart. After church, she would be likely seen hugging people, giving them words of love. She approached me at church shortly after my arrival at Fort Polk in 2000. I saw her coming in my direction and was actually trying to get away from her, hurriedly leaving after church service. Her purpose seemed to embrace people and love all over them, but I did not know her well at that point and chose to run instead. She said, "Gal, I know you are not trying to get out of here without giving me a hug."

Shucks, I thought. Reluctantly, I hugged her. Thank God, she did not give up on me because that beautiful-spirited woman of God is a joy to know. I am eternally grateful that God blessed us with a lifetime of friendship and be sisters at heart.

Sometime later, Niecey told me of a dream she had about me. She said that after the pastor preached, he did an altar call. I went to the altar for prayer, but she stayed in her seat. As I kneeled at the altar, Niecey said she was trying to get to me; she felt she had to come to me but couldn't. She tried to get over the chairs that separated us. She said while I was at the altar, still faced down, I was lifted off the floor.

She said that while in midair, I turned around to face the congregation with outstretched arms. I said in a strong voice to the congregation, "Jesus is coming soon!" No sooner did I say that, she heard the trumpets sound and saw visions of chariots on the wall. I was then turned back around toward the pulpit and, in a praying posture, placed back down at the altar. She said that all she kept saying was "Lord, thank you for letting me be a seer." A Google search reveals that chariots are symbolic of power and glory. God is glorious and powerful. Scripture states that "When a man went to inquire of God, he spake, 'Come, and let us go to the seer; for he that is now called a Prophet was before time called a seer'" (1 Sam. 9:9). Prophetess Niecey spoke what the Lord said.

The Palm of His Hand

HHC, 1st Infantry Division
Wurzburg, Germany (May 2, 2004)

My consistent prayer is that God would keep my family and me in the palm of his hands where nothing could pluck us out (John 10:28). I pray specific prayers because while I was a member at Resurrection Life Worship Center (RLWC), I had befriended Minister Irene who was a powerful prayer warrior. I remember telling her that I did not know how to pray. She said something that stuck with me to this day. She said, "Pray the word." I never forgot that and honed in on 2 Timothy 2:15: "Study to show thyself approved unto God, a workman that needeth not to be ashamed, rightly dividing the word of truth." That became my truth that in order for me to "pray" the word, I had to study the word; hence, my increased prayer life—I pray the word. When people tell me something referencing to the Bible, I would know truth from untruth. It is my belief that we put formalities into prayer. God instructs us how to pray by giving us the Lord's Prayer. We sometimes put more fluff in our prayer more than what is needed.

It is my belief and assurance that God indeed has me in the palm of his hands. This was my safety net, for come what may, God has me covered, and I am safe from dangers unawares.

In this dream, I saw myself sitting in the palm of a very large hand that was high over a large body of water; the hand never touched the water. With no knowledge as to how I got in the hand and over the body of water, confusion set in. While sitting in the palm of the hand, I could see that I was higher than the tall, large bridges ahead of us.

The hand began to move very fast across the water, but I never fell out of the hand; I just sat and watched, having no control of what came next. As the hand kept moving fast across the water with me sitting in it, I saw a bridge ahead, and it was clear that sitting that high over the water, the hand would undoubtedly crash into the bridge.

Surprisingly, as we approached the large and high bridge, the hand did not decrease in speed but dipped below, under, and back above to clear the bridge. I am still sitting in the palm of the hand as we went under the bridge. As soon as we cleared the bridge, the hand rose again to the same level as before and continued to move fast across the water.

The same thing happened again with another bridge that we came upon, but the hand never touched the bridge nor the water; it went under, below, and back up above. I felt safe because I was safe in the palm of his hand (John 10:28–29; Isa. 49:16). God's Word is true; he will do just what he said he would do. He answers prayers; God answers my prayers, and I know he will do the same for you if you just ask him. "We have not because we ask not" (James 4:2).

CHAPTER 4

God Speaks to Us Audibly

Army Enlistment

August 1984

I worked at DuPont in Goose Creek, South Carolina, for four years. DuPont paid very well, but DuPont rotated shifts weekly: 8:00 a.m. to 4:00 p.m. for seven days, 4:00 p.m. to 12:00 a.m. for seven days, and 12:00 a.m. to 8:00 a.m. for seven days. We also worked on weekends and holidays. It cost too much for the plant to shut down and start back up, so employees worked around the clock. We were off one weekend a month. The only shift that appealed to me was the eight-to-four shifts. Midnight shifts, especially, were most challenging; for it was hard for me to get sound sleep while taking care of two small children. I did not like shift rotations and had enough; I am done with shift rotations. Four years were more than enough for me, and the decision to enlist into the Army was the best choice for me.

While on the Greyhound Bus headed to Fort Jackson's Military Enlisted Processing Station (MEPS) to enlist into the Army, the Holy Spirit spoke audibly to me. "Now they are going to try to make you a Military Police [MP]. If you don't want to be an MP, say you don't want to be an MP." Becoming an MP was the furthest thing from my mind; I had had enough shift rotations while working at DuPont. Being an MP was not going to happen as far as I was concerned. I did not come from a military background, but I have seen MPs on TV, and what was assured that they worked outside mostly in all elements of weather, rain, snow, sleet, or hail, hot or cold; and they rotated shifts. Shift rotation was not an option for me—not even considered.

Upon arrival at MEPS, a recruiter asked what type of jobs I had considered. Finance was always appealing to me, and although I had no professional education or experience, the military's training in finance would surely set me up in becoming more of a better money manager in financial planning. I was very curious to learn about finance but did not pursue a finance career. I told the recruiter I was interested in finance.

The recruiter logged into his computer and said, "Sorry, no finance, but I have just the thing for you: *Military Police.*"

I quickly said, "I don't want to be an MP."

That did not deter him as he rambled on. "Wait a minute," he said. "You are the right height and the right built, and we need black females."

My voice projection went up as I said, "I do not want to be an MP!"

His insistence was unrelenting. "Before you say *no*, you can get a VA loan, and you can get free education."

Adamant, I said, "I do not want to be an MP!"

"Just look at the MP video first," he said.

Of which I appeased him and saw some wonderful things that MPs did. I said, "I do not want to be an MP!"

He had someone else come and talk to me. I felt that I was being interrogated and began to get highly annoyed. We went into another room and saw some more beautiful things that MPs do. I had enough, and my mood went from annoyed to downright angry. With folded arms, I repeated, "I do not want to be an MP!"

With my arms still folded and speaking with conviction and authority, I said, "I don't want to be an MP, and I don't want to be in this man's Army. I want to go home! I have a five o'clock bus to catch back to Charleston, and if I miss my bus, someone will take me home *today*! I want to go home!" It was then that the scurrying began; the recruiter hurried back to his computer and said, "We have just the thing for you: Administrative Specialist."

Thank God for the Holy Spirit and for me paying attention to that sweet, still voice that whispered in my ears. This was the beginning of a very rewarding military career. The experiences with my military family and forever friends, sisterhood/brotherhood, discipline, training, and leadership are etched in my heart forever.

The Called: Who, Me?

HHC, VII Corps Stuttgart, Germany
February 1987

Sometimes, God speaks to us clearly to give us wake-up calls, a reality check. There are times when we are in denial of things we may not want to believe. We may make excuses to justify our actions and make us feel better for why we did what was done or did not do something in particular. In this case, the realization was, I made excuses to justify my actions because they made me feel better. I realize that now.

Throughout my formative years, I learned one of the most popular scriptures that pastors, leaders, and Sunday school teachers often taught. John 4:14–18 speaks of how Jesus met a woman at the well and told her about herself. Jesus told her to go get her husband, of which the woman said she has no husband. Jesus's response was that she has had five husbands, and the one she has now was not her own. This experience begins.

I went to the local church on the military installation under the tutelage of Pastor Morgan. That particular Sunday, we had a guest speaker, an elderly white man. I don't remember the sermon, but I remembered his prophecy. During that time in my life, I was not studying God's Word that much, but accounts of childhood scriptures came into remembrance. Still, biblical days, I thought, were different from what we experience nowadays. People whom I have never met don't know me; therefore, they could not speak into my life or tell me about "me." That was my thought process at that time.

After the sermon, the pastor (guest speaker) asked anyone who wanted prayer to make a row down the aisle. Four females were last in line; I was the fourth female. The pastor laid hands on the first of the four females' forehead as he spoke about the problems in her life. She let out a scream, hollered, cried, and fell to the floor. I talk to God just like I talk to other people in my life. I looked up and said, "Oh, Lord, don't tell me we have one of them." When I say *them*, I mean someone who speaks into someone else's life about things done or to come. At that stage in my life, I did not have any known problems, so I said, "Lord, if this man tells me in front of your congregation about problems that I don't have, I will have to correct him." Ushers lifted her from the floor, and the pastor went to the next person.

The pastor laid his hand on the forehead of the second female and spoke of what was not right in her life and other things. She screamed and fell down, crying. I looked up and said, "Lord, this doesn't make sense. How can he tell people what's going on with them? He doesn't know us." He laid hands on the third female and made a similar prophecy. While he spoke to the lady in front of me, I looked up toward heaven and said, "Lord, you know me and my mouth. If I have a problem, I do not know that it is a problem. If he tells me about my problems in front of your congregation, I have to correct him." The lady let out a holler, cried, and eventually fell to the floor. While they were picking her up from the floor, I looked up and said, "Well, Lord, I'm next. Here I go."

I did not want to hear the what I called foolishness that this pastor was saying to others, and now he stood in front of me, paused briefly, and said, "My child, you're an angel. The Lord's got work for you to do!" He lifted my arms in the air, and I stood there, dumbfounded. I was expecting him to tell me about the problems in my life that I didn't have much, like he said to the others before me. Anything else he said became a blur to me because of his prophecy of God having work for me to do. I just stood there, wondering, *What just happened here?*

After I sat down trying to process what just happened, suddenly I became angered as I said sternly to myself, "Pastor Morgan told him to say that!"

Then I heard a soft voice whisper in my right ear, saying, "Why you?"

I thought about that because Pastor Morgan had no way of knowing that I would be going up for prayer that became prophecy. I calmed down immediately. I wondered what work God had for me to do. How would I know, and how long would it take me to know? I had no idea that God was already working in and through me and would continue to refine me to be how "he" wanted me to be for his will.

Years later, I told my girlfriend Dee about the prophecy. She asked if I ever stopped to think that maybe God was talking about me as the problem. I did not think about myself being associated with "the problem"; I honestly did not think I had a problem and especially that I would "be the problem." I must admit, I was sure that the pastor would have told me about my nonexistent problems, as he did with the three females before me, but instead, he (God) had a message for me. This experience was so significant that it ministered to my spirit, for you see, I was the Samaritan woman. I was seeing a married man, and he was not my own. God showed me the errors of my ways and wanted to use me, but I had to be cleansed. If God wanted to use me, I had to let go of some things that I was doing that were not pleasing unto him. Thank God for the revelation. Second Timothy 2:21 reminds us that "if a man purges himself from these, he shall be a vessel unto honor, sanctified, and meet for the master's use, and prepared unto every good work." God had work for me to do, but he had to clean me up. "Speak, Lord, for thy servant heareth" (1 Sam. 3:10).

Mr. Archer: Angels Unaware

Tampa, Florida
June 1999

"Be not forgetful to entertain strangers: for thereby some have entertained angels unawares" (Heb. 13:2).

My military obligations took me to the 3rd Infantry Division, Fort Stewart, Georgia, as my first assignment after Warrant Officer School in late 1995. While in the Warrant Officer Basic Course (WOBC), I, along with another inbound warrant officer, was interviewed for a position at MacDill AFB, Tampa, Florida. The assignment was for Fort Stewart with duty at MacDill AFB. They wanted someone who got along well with people, worked independently, would represent the organization well, and was personable, along with other attributes necessary to work on a four-star-general-commanded installation. I was the chosen warrant officer.

The latter part of my three-and-a-half-year assignment at MacDill, I was about to earn my Master's Degree in Human Resources Management. About six weeks before I was to relocate to Seoul, Korea, while sitting on a bench overlooking Tampa Bay studying for my final exam, an old man walked up to me and started talking. He said hello, and I said hello. In my mind, I was saying, *Go away, old man. I am trying to study.*

He said, "I see you are studying."

I said, "Yes, I am studying for my final exam." I said again in my mind, *Please go away, old man.*

He asked if I was in the military; of which I said, "Yes, I am headed to Korea in about a month." He asked if I had children; of which I said, "Two."

"Married?"

"Divorced."

"Who will keep your children while you are in Korea?"

"My sister, Sylvia, who is in the Air Force (AF) will keep them."

Although his line of questioning seemed somewhat personal, I took no offense. "How old are they? Where are you from?"

"SC," I said. I closed my book; I knew I was not going to study.

The old man smiled and asked why I stopped to talk to him. I said, "I read somewhere in the Bible, 'Beware of who you entertain for you could be entertaining angels unaware' Hebrews 13:2." He smiled again. I said, "And you are an old man."

He wanted to know why I called him old.

As politely as possible, I replied, "Because your speech was slurred and you moved slowly."

He introduced himself as Archer, Basil Archer. He talked some more about his son and daughter whom he felt did not appreciate all he had done to help them as adults. He just kept talking and smiling, and I listened attentively. It actually felt good talking to Mr. Archer.

Mr. Archer chuckled as he reminisced about how he used to hang out with Ray Charles. We laughed at some of the stories he told about their friendship, of how Ray Charles saw shadows and how Ray Charles shaved. He talked a lot about Ray Charles and said he, himself, used to be a boxer from the Caribbean. The other part of the conversation seemed to be a blur, but the meeting was for a lifetime of cherished memories for me. Before the conversation ended, Mr. Archer gave me his business card and said that if my children needed anything, I should tell my sister to let him know.

Over the years, while assigned overseas or stateside, Mr. Archer and I exchanged phone calls and wrote letters. I always smiled when I saw a scribbled, handwritten letter from Mr. Archer, and he was faithful in writing. My cousin Nita said I helped to make an old man's last years on earth very pleasant and enjoyable.

While assigned to Fort Polk, Louisiana, after my tour in Korea, Mr. Archer called; we laughed and talked as we did before. We had a one-time face-to-face meeting while at Tampa Bay. About two years after my arrival to Fort Polk, Mr. Archer and I had a long conversation. He said, "You are from SC, right?"

I said, "Yes, indeed."

He said, "I am going to purchase two acres of land for you in SC. That should be enough."

I said, "I don't want to talk about land. How are you?"

He said he was in the hospital, that the cancer was back, and I was shocked. "Mr. Archer, you never told me you had cancer."

He said, "Oh, child, I am not afraid." He knew his God.

"Mr. Archer, I am coming to see you."

He said, "I don't want you to see me like this."

"I'm coming," I said, "to see you."

I booked a flight within a few weeks with reservations to Tampa, Florida, to see Mr. Archer. His daughter was to pick me up from the airport, but she was a no-show. A former soldier picked me up from the airport and let me stay at her place. We tried unsuccessfully to find Mr. Archer. Hospitals did not have him as a patient; fearing the worse, we started calling mortuaries. Mr. Archer did not make it out of the hospital; one of the mortuaries did have his remains.

I told the mortician that I was not family by bloodline, but I was in the Army and came to see Mr. Archer but did not get there in time. I explained that we kept in touch throughout my military assignments, but he recently told me that he was in the hospital. I wondered if he would be so kind as to give me an obituary. He took my info and sent me several obituaries. My spirit rejoiced that he was not suffering. Mr. Archer sent this poem to me while in Korea and left me with this very cherished memory. This poem ministered to my spirit, and hopefully, it will minister to yours as well.

I Wish You Enough
(author unknown)

I wish you enough faith for you to "stand"
I wish your generosity would be reciprocated unto you
I wish you enough strength to bear your cross
I wish you prosperity beyond measures
I wish you an abundant life
I wish that you lacked for nothing

I wish complete restoration of your health
I wish your "little" become a "lot"
I simply wish you enough of everything good that life has to offer.

Scripture states, "Beloved, I wish above all things that thou prosper and be in health as thy soul prospereth" (3 John 1:2). Thank you, God, for allowing Mr. Archer and my path to cross and develop a friendship while leaving me with cherished memories.

Try the Spirit by the Spirit

Resurrection Life Worship Center (RLWC)
Fort Polk, LA
April 2001

My membership into the Resurrection Life Worship Center (RLWC) was an awakening for me. My prayers have always been that God will let his light radiate and shine so bright within me that when people see me, they see the Spirit of Christ working in and through me.

The first Sunday of my attendance at the RLWC, with closed eyes and arms raised, I ushered in God's presence to speak to me. That day is still fresh in my mind. I wore a red double-breasted pants suit and sat in the third row. Early in the service, the first lady looked at me from the pulpit and said, "Sister, you have the Spirit of the Lord all over you." I looked around because, surely, she was not talking to me because this was my first day in attendance; she did not know me, but she knew the Holy Spirit. She pointed at me and said, "Yes, you, sister in red. You have the Spirit of the Lord all over you." The Lord was in my heart and in this place; there's no need to look any further for a church home.

On Easter Sunday, the leaders put on an Easter rendition of the crucifixion. That day will forever be etched in my mind and in my heart. I sat in the back at the beginning of a row next to the aisle where the cast of the play had to pass to get to the front. That was a long walk from the back of the building to the front, and the person who played Jesus carried a large cross on his back, hunched over with the weight of the world as depicted with the heavy cross. Reflecting on my Lord and Savior Jesus Christ's long walk in my mind to his crucifixion, tears streamed down my face uncontrollably.

The depiction was so surreal. As the person who played Jesus got closer to me, he was hunched over with the cross and looked up at me with my tear-streaked face. I looked down at him and was not able to restrain myself from the sadness of what they were doing to my Lord. The face that looked back at me up close and personal was not the person in the play; he had a long beard with warm and compassionate eyes. That is the vision that flashed before my eyes; I declare before my God, when he looked up at me with sad eyes, his spirit leapt into my body and our spirits fused together. My body jerked and was knocked slightly off balance from that fusion. That was an awesome experience. Scripture tells us to test the spirit to know if it is of God (1 John 4:1). Thank you, Lord, for living in me and me in you.

CHAPTER 5

God Speaks to Us through Confirmations

Fort Riley, Kansas
February 1985

My first military duty assignment after Basic Training (BT) was HHC 1st Infantry Division at Fort Riley, Kansas. I was a young Private First Class (PFC) with two children. My children were with my mom until I got settled in Kansas. It took a little longer to get housing because in order to get on the housing wait list, I would have to be a Specialist (SPC), the next higher rank. Therefore, I had to find an affordable place off the army installation until I was promoted and added to the housing wait list. Our salaries as PFCs were very low, and I could not afford a down payment to rent a trailer. As God would have it, a friend invited me to bingo. I do not like bingo, but she badgered me, and I went. That night, I won $500; I had never won anything before. That was my deposit for the trailer. Oh, happy day!

I had to get my children who were in South Carolina. My blessed sister at heart and dear friend, Sandra #1 (affectionately called because she is older than me) from DuPont would often call to check on me. After small talks, I would cry and say, "I want my children." She must have heard one of my sobbing stories one time too many as I cried, "I want my children!" She would try to comfort me by letting me know I will get my children. One day, I told Sandra #1 that I missed my children so much, and I wanted them. I began to cry. Sandra #1 said, "Hayes, don't cry. You will get your children."

Look how God works. Sandra #1, who lived in Summerville, jumped in her SUV, went to Hollywood, picked up my children, and brought them to me in Kansas. When she arrived to my trailer, with that spirit of humility, she said, "Hayes, it's just not fair. The closer I got to Kansas, somebody moved the sign back." We still laugh about that today. That was a long drive from South Carolina to Kansas. Her devoted husband flew to Kansas the next day and drove back to Summerville. They would not take any money for their acts of kindness. To God be the glory for the things he has done. I pray that God will pour back into them in abundance, hundredfold, above and beyond measure, and in overflow for that which they poured out in love and kindness. This is a sterling example of the scripture in Proverbs 18:24: "A man that hath friends must show himself friendly: and there is a friend that sticketh closer than a brother. I believe that I am as much of a friend to her as she is to me." She showed me the essence of what a friend is; I am humbled and very appreciative. What is the cost for kindness? Priceless! Their acts of kindness will be remembered for a lifetime.

Listen to the "Message"

HHC, 1st Infantry Division
Wurzburg, Germany
November 2003

Victory through Faith (VTF) was the local church I attended in Wurzburg, Germany. Our pastor was a powerful man of God who preached fervently, and the Spirit of Christ moved in the building. Pastor was about to do a Permanent Change of Station (PCS) for the military, and Pastor Mason, a younger pastor, was going to be our new pastor. I had heard Pastor Mason preach before, and he was awesome, coming from a lineage of pastors in his family. When I heard that he would be the new VTF pastor, sadly, I looked at the man and did not pay attention to the message. I thought to myself, *He is the same age as my daughter. I am not going to stay here.* I refused to listen to our new pastor specifically because of his age; forgive me, Lord. I, therefore, attended another church.

My choice to drive two hours every week from Wurzburg, Germany, to Sembach, Germany, was twofold. My sister was assigned to Sembach AFB; and her pastor, in his awesomeness, was older. Church services, coupled with family time, were worth the trip that is until the snow started to fall. A two-hour commute to go to church was no longer appealing. The resolve to see my sister from time to time was doable, and my attendance with VTF was reconsidered. Pastor Mason was dynamic in sermon delivery, but he was so young, and that was the only reason I chose not to become a member of VTF.

Once winter approached, bringing with it lots of snow, I went back to our local church, VTF. Around that time, I had been praying earnestly that God would make me more of a powerful and effective prayer warrior, praying for any given situation or circumstance. The first Sunday that I attended VTF, we had a guest speaker. He was a small black man, had a dark beard, and unpacked a powerful message. Afterward, he did an altar call and prophesied to those of us who came up for prayer.

I went up to the altar along with my friend CPT Hayes. She was standing to my right as the pastor prophesied to her. I had my hands lifted in the air with my eyes closed to focus on God and to block out surrounding distractions. The pastor stopped in front of CPT Hayes, laid hands on her, and spoke into her life. As he moved in front of me, I opened my eyes and followed his eyes to my left ring finger. In my mind, I said, *Oh, Lord, please don't let him say I was praying for a husband because that was not my prayer.* He stood there in front of me, and then he said with a strong voice, "I saw you before I came into this church this morning." He paused and said, "*I* [pointing to himself] saw *you* [pointing to me] before I came into this church [pointing down to the floor] this morning." He paused again and said with more conviction while pointing to himself then to me, "*I* saw *you* before I came into this church this morning!" Then he clapped his hands three times, and with an authoritative voice, he said, "You are not hearing me!" While pointing to himself and then to me, he said strongly, "*I* saw *you* before I came into *this church…this morning*!" He said in a more calm voice, "God said you're doing what you are supposed to be doing… just pray," and he walked off. God is so awesome! Out of anything that the pastor could have said to me, he spoke my prayer request to God; I did not hesitate to become a member of VTF. Amen and Amen!

A Witness for the Lord

Navy Base Exchange (BX)
Norfolk, Virginia
June 2015

Our testimonies, our truth of an event that happened, is not necessarily for us. We know how our outcome ended. Our testimonies, therefore, may be for someone else to give him or her hope or encouragement for whatever strife they may have encountered in life. My dear friend Diva believes in God but rarely attends church services. In my heart, it is my belief that this particular experience was to show her God at work and a confirmation for me.

During that time, my prayers to God were that he would let his light radiate and shine so bright within me that when people see me, they see the Spirit of Christ working in and through me. I also prayed that he would continue to bless and anoint me that I may motivate, encourage, and inspire others and to put a host of guardian angels around my entire family and me, protecting us everywhere we go and in everything that we do.

Diva asked me to go with her and Rosa to look for an item that was hard to find locally but was advertised at the Navy Base Exchange (BX) in Norfolk, Virginia. Norfolk was over two hours away. Each time she asked me to go, my response was *no*. After much badgering that I don't go anywhere with them, I conceded and went. Shopping is not my forte, but I purchased a few items. I went to the first register that was attended by a lady who was seemingly in her late sixties or early seventies. Diva and Rosa went to nearby registers.

The cashier looked at me and smiled. She said, "I can tell you love the Lord."

Without hesitation and with strong conviction, I said with joy, "I sure do!"

She continued, "You know, the people in my church think I am a prophetess, but I see myself more of a seer." Then she said, "You know, you are going to motivate, encourage, and inspire others."

I looked up toward heaven and said, "Lord, I know I didn't hear what I thought I just heard."

I looked back at her as she said, "You are going to go through some things, but you are going to motivate, encourage, and inspire others." She moved her head, looking to my left and then to my right as she said, "Hmmm, I see an angel on your left, and I see an angel on your right." I said, "Oh, my God!" At that exact moment, Diva called my name. The cashier said, "She doesn't even know what we are talking about." I tried to shake her hand, but our hands never touched.

As I walked to Diva, she said, "You were holding up the line," of which I said, "There was no one else in the line." She assured me that someone was standing in that line from the moment I walked up to the register. My response was of surprise because no one whimpered, moved, nor said a word; it was just the cashier and me. It felt as if we were in a time capsule where time stood still; there was a sense of peace, calm, and total euphoria.

Diva probed by asking me what the lady said to me.

I told Diva, "The lady said she could tell that I love the Lord and that I would motivate, encourage, and inspire others. She also said she saw an angel to my left and an angel to my right."

She asked, "Why did that lady say that to you?"

I responded, "She said she saw Christ in me."

She continued with "I thought you knew her."

With glee in my voice, I said, "I have never seen that lady before in my life."

My spirit rejoiced because of anything that the cashier could have said to me, she told me confirmatively those three prayer requests I was sending up to the Lord. "Use me, Lord. Use me." Additionally, Diva witnessed God at work with a confirmation from a stranger. Her experience reminded me of the passage in 2 Kings 6:17, "Open her eyes that she might see him at work."

My Nephew (Shawn)

December 2005

I often pray that God would make me a fisher of men (Matt. 4:19), drawing others unto him to be saved, delivered, and set free. I strive to be a vessel of honor, sanctified, and meet for the Master's use and prepared unto all good works (2 Tim. 2:21). Use me, Lord, for I am available unto you.

Shawn was kind, considerate, and very caring. He was loved, but he was also dealing with internal issues that I summed up as rejection, dejection, a need to feel accepted, and a sense of belonging. My son was eleven months older than Shawn. Whenever I went home for a visit when Shawn was younger, we would talk; I think he needed to unpack things that were bothering him. It may have been a cry for help. He had such a humble spirit. My oldest brother, Vernon, who is now deceased, told me that Leon, a former brother-in-law, said he was going to kill Shawn. Vernon told Leon that if he ever hurt Shawn, he would come after him. Based on my brother's statement, I personally filed a police report for a very serious incident that happened later when Leon physically assaulted Shawn.

My son and other younger cousins who were visiting were with Shawn before the incident happened. Shawn and his cousins were going outside when Leon asked Shawn where he was going. Shawn said, "Outside."

Leon grabbed his arm, and Shawn pulled it away, saying, "Get your hand off me."

Leon dragged Shawn into the bedroom and slammed the door. The other children stood outside the door as they heard the cry, "Help, he's going to kill me! Help, he's going to kill me!"

Travis, his older brother in his late teens at that time, was in the kitchen, not knowing what was happening to his younger brother in the bedroom. Someone must have alerted him because Travis busted the door in to protect his brother. Shawn was gasping for air with Leon's hand around his throat while swinging the hard-soled shoe over Shawn's face and body. Travis and Leon wrestled. Travis, in his anger, is not one to play with.

Travis grabbed a nearby bat, and Leon ran from Travis's grip.

Sheri, my niece, vividly recalls the assault. She was under the hair dryer in the kitchen when Travis and the older cousins started to run. Shortly thereafter, she ran to see what the commotion was about. She saw the cousins trying to break up the fight between Travis and Leon when Shawn stumbled out of the room. She thought Shawn was wearing a red shirt but soon realized that he was covered in his blood. Shawn's eyes rolled to the back of his head, and he collapsed at her feet. Travis picked Shawn up and took him to Mama's house. Sheri looked in the room and found blood spatters from the ceiling to the floor and a broken wooden shoe that Leon used in the assault against Shawn. Blood was strewed all over the place. In all fairness, my sister had no idea what was happening at her house because we were at Mom's house at the time of the assault.

When Travis brought Shawn to Mama's house, he was angry. My sister, mom, other relatives, and I came out of the house when Travis arrived with Shawn.

The first words I heard my sister say to her son was, "What have you done now?"

I went off. "What do you mean what has he done? Look at your son! Shawn could not have done anything that bad to be abused like this. Look at your son! The question is, what are you going to do?"

"I don't know yet," she said.

I said, "Since you don't know yet what you are going to do, I know what I am going to do."

I went into the house and called the police. The policeman would not take the report of the assault because I was not the guardian or the parent, and I did not witness the assault. I told the policeman that I did not see the actual abuse as it unfolded, but I saw the aftereffects of the beating. I saw the bloodstained towel and Shawn's swollen face. It was about that time when my sister walked into the room and asked what I was doing.

I put the receiver closer to my mouth and said loudly so the policeman could hear clearly, "Since you don't know what you are going to do about your son who was just assaulted, I called the police."

The policeman said, "Ma'am, I will take this report."

My intent to file that police report was twofold to rule out any potential future allegations if it was said that Shawn was a runaway when, in actuality, his absence may have been because of harm or death. I wanted that report on file for a full-fledged investigation if needed.

Shawn would ask to come live with me repeatedly, which I thought was a great idea. He and Trey would have grown up together in a military environment, but as an active-duty soldier, that could not happen without guardianship paperwork, of which I never received. As life threw more punches at Shawn, who was now a mid to late teenager did not want to come live with me. He had joined a gang. He eventually wanted out of the gang, but that was not an option—alive, that is.

Throughout my military years, I faithfully wrote letters to Shawn. He did not write back, but since things were the way it was, I wanted him to know the Lord. Each letter would have some encouraging words and messages about the Lord in the hopes that he would develop a personal relationship with the Lord for himself. This was important because I want to be reunited with my loved ones in heaven when we cease to exist here on earth.

The last time I saw my dear sweet Shawn alive, he was in jail. My sister, Sylvia, and I visited Shawn on our return from overseas assignments. We arrived after visiting hours, but since we were in the military, they allowed us to see him only for fifteen minutes. We talked through a glass window. I can still feel Shawn's love and hear his voice.

He said, "Auntie, I love you."

I said, "I love you too, Shawn."

He put his right hand on the glass window, and I put my hand in his hand on the glass window, and our eyes locked lovingly as he said, "Auntie… I love you!"

I said, "I love you too, my dear Shawn." Who would have known that would be the last time I would see Shawn alive.

I kept writing, though. I told Shawn that if something should happen to him and if God blesses him with his last breath to say anything, do not call his mom because his mom could not help him. Do not call Auntie because Auntie could not help him. Call on the name of the Lord; ask God for forgiveness for anything you may have done that was wrong and make your peace with him. Glory! Hallelujah! Praise God! Shawn was twenty-two years old when he died in December 2005. I was unable to attend Shawn's homegoing service because of a diagnosed heart condition, of which surgery was required the next week. Shawn was shot at close range in the chest. I rejoice because the story that came to me was that his friends rushed him to the hospital. He pulled out his cell phone and said, "Give this to Katie" (his girlfriend). He said, "Tell Baby G [his son] I love him." Then he started talking to God. "Praise your holy name. Thank you, Lord, for being the God of second chances." With Shawn's last breath, he called on the name of the Lord, and he made peace with God—confirmation. I know Shawn is in heaven worshiping you Oh, Holy One!

We never know what a person would truly do if their anger or hatred were deep-rooted. Sometimes we are blinded by love or an illusion of what love feels like for our significant other. It is my belief that we should keep our children's well-being first. Love is not supposed to hurt. Healing begins when we ask God for forgiveness and forgive ourselves.

CHAPTER 6

Obedience Is Better Than Sacrifice

Trey

Goose Creek, South Carolina
November 1982

If we stop long enough to listen to God as he speaks to us, we could save ourselves from anguish, guilt, regrets, or hurt that may follow when something tragic or undesirable happens. If only we had listened. It is my belief that sometimes, our fear of the Lord makes us grow up fast and strengthens our daily walk with God. The fear of the Lord is the beginning of knowledge (Prov. 1:7). But thank God for obedience. "To obey is better than sacrifice" (1 Sam. 15:22).

With the birth of my son in September 1982 came an overwhelming love for him that was so strong it scared me. "Thou shalt have no other gods before me" (Exod. 20:3). "For God is a jealous God" (Exod. 20:5). My greatest fear was that my love for Trey was so disconcerting that I feared God would be jealous and would take him from me. I kept telling God that I love "him" more than I love Trey. Those episodes of telling God that he was first in my life were as if it fell on deaf ears.

I had more episodes of that same overwhelming love for Trey, all the while telling God that my love for Trey was not stronger than my love for him. The fear of the Lord was overpowering. Those episodes of overwhelming love for Trey finally took its toll on me. Trey was almost two months old when I had yet another episode of telling God I loved him more than I loved Trey. I did not want God to take my son away from me because I may have put Trey before him. "God, I don't love Trey more than I love you. I love you more, Lord!"

During one of those episodes, I heard the Spirit of the Lord ask, "Who are you trying to convince, me or you?" His voice was audible, strong, clear, and frightening because God is God; it was God's truth, so it was true. I didn't think hard on that because upon searching my heart, my realization was that I was trying to convince myself that I love God more than I love Trey. That scared me to life…

It was very late at night when the realization of not placing God first in my life came to light; my fear of the Lord was so great that I took action. I grabbed my son, ran outside, and lifted him over my head with outstretched arms toward heaven. With a loud voice and speaking with conviction, I said, "Lord, unto you I give my son!" Immediately, I saw a vision of a forefinger that touched my forehead. The touch was as a light, feathery feeling that went from the top of my head to the sole of my feet. I felt peace and calm; it was so soothing, comforting, and reassuring.

To this day, I have never had an overwhelming love for Trey, and I have not felt fearful that God would take him. Trey was dedicated to God that night when he was a baby, and come what may, God has him in the palm of his hands. "The fear of the Lord is the beginning of wisdom and the knowledge of the Holy is understanding" (Prov. 9:10).

Daddy, I Forgive You

HHC, 1st Infantry Division
Fort Riley, Kansas
February 1985

God, I can't thank you enough for obedience. When I think about how God saved me from myself, how he purged, cleansed, and washed me from my unforgiving spirit, my soul cries, "Hallelujah!" From childhood, the harbored resentment toward my dad would have hindered what God had in store for me. God cannot work in a heart that is full of junk or stuff that is not of him. He needs a willing heart. "Speak Lord, for your servant heareth" (1 Sam. 3:10).

My dad left when I was about six years old. His memory was all that I had, besides the fact that we looked alike, and with other people's reminders over the years telling me that I act just like him. My dad had deep dimples with a very beautiful smile. He was charming, very handsome, charismatic, and loved to laugh; he was a practical joker. I can see him laughing at a joke he thought was funny but frightening for me as a child. He was getting groceries out of the trunk of his car. I was willing to help, so I asked if there were any more groceries. He smiled and said, "Why don't you go and see?" I jumped in the trunk for a bag, and he slammed the trunk on me. He did not let me stay there long, but he sure was laughing. I was not laughing and was rather frightened; it was so dark in the trunk.

One day, my dad left to go to the store and never came back; he made a new life for himself in New York. My heart told me that if we (children) were not here, he would not have left; that was my belief that stayed with me. I told Sylvia what I felt at that time, although it escapes her memory. Still, my childhood was very happy because of a loving mom. Mom did not have much to give, but with what she had, she gave us *all* of it—her heart, love, and support; she gave us *herself*.

Sometimes I could not help but think about Dad. As a child, there was an old gospel song that I sang a lot when I heard it on the radio. A woman was singing to God and thanking him for her miracle. The tune is embedded in my heart even now, but I can only remember a verse: "To see my father's face again, look at the miracle. Oh, thank you, Jesus. You are a miracle God, miracle God. Oh, you set me free. Thank you for working my miracle. Oooh, thank you, Jesus!"

As I reflected on my childhood, my heart sang for my dad. Although we never spoke of him, my heart longed for him with reminders from my heart that if we were not here existing, our dad would not have left. The constant reminder of Dad came from Mom, not in reminiscence of him but in disciplining me. I am the oldest of my dad's children by marriage. As a child, I knew most of the whippings I received were not for me; it was for my dad. Mom would whip me for some of the silliest things: "Didn't I tell you to keep your hands out of the dishwater?" I was only washing dishes that my siblings did not seemingly like to do. "Who said you could have a peanut-butter-and-jelly sandwich?" When she whipped my butt, she would be saying, "Just like your daddy, just like your daddy." It did not help that I looked just like him, acted like him, and was a practical joker just like him. I did not hold that against Mom; as a child, I understood that much. I was his constant reminder. I clung to Mom, though, and she didn't let me go.

I assumed that my dad had been making contact with Mom in the years to come. When I was in the twelfth grade, Mom pulled all of her children together for a talk. She said, "Your daddy wants to come back. Who wants him to come back?" Two people said *no*, and I was one of the two. Majority won, but I think what really sealed the deal was Jan saying, "At least you will be with your own husband and not someone else." I wanted to rip Jan's tongue out of her mouth for saying that to Mom. Although true, I imagined the hurt Mom must have felt and did what she felt was right for everyone; she took him back. I make no excuses for Mom's actions, but at that time, she did what she felt she had to do with ten children under her roof.

Dad came back home, and I was not happy. Within thirty days of him being back home, Mom came to me and said, "I can't believe your daddy. I just took him back, and he had the nerve to say why don't him and I go get an apartment and leave you all in the house!" What reeled through my mind was, "Can you say *confirmation*?" My childhood thoughts came flooding back; if we were not here, he would not have left. Rage took over, and I did not receive him well.

Mom tried to get us (Dad and me) to connect but to no avail. For dinner, Mom would say, "Sandra, go ask your daddy if he wants to eat?" Unlike the others, the word *daddy* never came out of my mouth, for I would go to him, face-to-face, and say in a harsh tone, "Mama wanna know if you want to eat." Other times, my dad took measures in his own hand.

"Why can't you call me daddy? Sylvia calls me daddy, Junie calls me daddy, Gail calls me daddy, and Kenneth calls me daddy. Why can't you call me daddy?"

"Because I don't feel it in my heart, and until I do, you will never hear me call you daddy! Oh, by the way, when I give Mama a Father's Day card, don't say anything to me because I don't know what you woulda, coulda, shoulda done because you weren't here!"

Another time, he approached me and said, "I don't think I like you."

Flippantly, I said, "Well, Daddy dearest, why do you think you do not like me?"

He said in a sharp tone, "Because you remind me too much of me!"

"Well then," I replied, "since I remind you too much of you, is it safe to say you don't like yourself?" I was just so darn angry and never once asked myself why. Every action with him was a reaction from me. Kathy, our first cousin who grew up in our house, would say, "I feel so sorry for Sam."

"Why would you feel sorry for him?" was my immediate comeback. I was unrelenting toward him. I was bold and not afraid.

For years, I was on defense with him. If I was to be true to my heart, I was angry, bitter, resentful, miserable, and hateful; *hate* is a strong word but could not be overruled if the truth is told. As more time went by, rather than calling him daddy, we would have a confrontation about my behavior. The word *daddy* would not be sincere if spoken from me, so why say it? Now that I think about it, I honestly cannot remember my dad calling my name since he came back—ever. I'm almost certain he saw my pain but did not know how to deal with it. God began to work on me when my dad and my brother Kenneth were wrestling playfully, as in professional wrestling on television. My brother had Dad in a hold, Dad kicked his leg to get free, and his small toe caught the end of the couch and broke. My heart hurt to see him in pain from the injury, but not enough to get mushy.

In 1980, Dad marched me down the aisle for my wedding; it was the right thing to do for Mom's sake. I did not have to see him often since I would be in my own place. August 17, 1984, was my enlistment in the Army. My first duty assignment after Basic Training (BT) and Advanced Individual Training (AIT) for our job was at Fort Riley, Kansas, with an arrival in February 1985. One night in March 1985, I was on my bed, lying on my left side, watching television, when I felt two slaps on my right cheek (butt), and the Spirit of the Lord said, "Write your daddy!" I looked toward heaven and said, "Lord, what am I going to say!? I have nothing to say to that man!" The thought of writing Dad was totally dismissed without a second thought.

On April 1985, I was once again lying on my bed, and the same thing happened; only this time, the two slaps on my butt was harder, and the Spirit of the Lord's voice was stern, "Write your daddy!"

"Lord, what am I going to say to that man! I have nothing to say to him!" In obedience, I picked up my long stenographer notepad and began to write. The long stenographer notepad on my bed would soon be filled with decades of feelings that described hurt, pain, anguish, bitterness, resentment, abandonment, and anything that came to my mind or out of my heart. I wrote and cried, wrote some more, and cried a lot. Each stroke of my pen was met with lots of tears. It's as if a floodgate opened, and it seems I was writing faster than I was thinking; actually, there was no thought. I just wrote what was poured in my spirit or maybe what had taken root in my heart.

I wrote seven pages, and in the last paragraph, I wrote with sincerity, "Daddy, I don't know why you left. I don't care why you left. We can't make up for lost times, but we can start from the present to be a family. I love you." My dad had finally breached my heart; he was very happy. Through the eyes of my sister Sylvia, who was at home with Daddy, she would describe how Daddy would read my letter, smile, fold it up, and put it back in his wallet. He would pull my letter out again, read it, smile, and put it back in his wallet. Mom asked what was in the letter, and he would tell her that was none of her business; it was for him. Sylvia told Daddy he did not have to tell her what was in the letter because she already knew. I told her what I had written.

Sylvia would give me the details of Daddy's last days. One of her classmates told her of a dream she had about Daddy standing on a pier, and a large boat was far away on the water. My dad kept saying, "I can't let that boat leave me. I can't let that boat leave me."

Sylvia said Daddy did something she never saw him do before; he read the Bible regularly. One day, he stood at the door and just looked around while absorbing everything in his view. She said Daddy's five brothers came by, which they had not done before; she thought they were going to get drunk. She went on her date, and when she came back, Daddy was on the floor. She thought he was drunk, but any beer that was in the refrigerator before she went on her date was there upon her return. Daddy had a stroke and a brain aneurysm. On May 10, 1985, less than one month after Daddy received my letter, he died.

God works in mysterious ways. I connected in heart with my dad for a short period of time, but his death stung. Many people came to our house during the bereavement period. I remember, as I made my way through people standing and talking in the living room, trying to get to the porch, I felt someone grab my hand. Through the crowd of people, I could not see who it was, but as I looked down, all I saw was a hand. Someone placed a blue card in my hand with a poem, "Let Go and Let God." The poem was so poignant that it ministered to my spirit in a profound way. I taped that blue card with the poem to my bedpost and read it every night before I went to sleep. For years, that poem traveled with me from one military assignment to the other. I knew it by heart. One day, my poem just disappeared off my bedpost; I guess it had served its purpose. That poem fed my spirit for so many years, and I pray that it would feed yours. When you read the poem, say it like you feel the essence of its meaning. Words can bring life, so speak life into these words.

Let Go and Let God

As children bring their broken toys
With tears for us to mend
I brought my broken dreams to God
Because he was my friend
But instead of leaving him, in peace, to
  work alone
I hung around and tried to help with ways
  that were my own
At last I snatched them back and cried,
  "How could you be so slow?"
"My child," he said, "what could I do?
You never did—let go."

Sometimes, we ask God to help us in our varied circumstances, but we try to work things out ourselves. He may not be moving fast enough for us, but in our season, we will see just how God did indeed work things out. The

"Let Go and Let God" poem is embedded in my heart, and every night at bedtime, I say that poem because it still ministers to my spirit as a reminder to give my problems to God and leave it there; that works for me.

I feel great that I hearkened to the prodding of God's voice to write to Daddy. I thank God for second chances and asked him to forgive me for not listening the first time he spoke to me. Hebrews 3:7–8 states, "Wherefore as the Holy Ghost saith, today if ye will hear his voice, harden not your hearts." My heart was hardened at first, but thank God for obedience; I now live with no regrets. I rejoice because my spirit was purged, cleansed, and washed from the negative energy of my daddy that stayed with me over the decades. I had the pleasure of meeting Daddy in my heart for about a month before he went home to glory; I am eternally grateful to God for allowing us to connect. Thank God for obedience!

Shortly after my daddy's death, I had a dream about him. He was lying on the floor. He had on all-white clothing and flashed a great big, beautiful smile at me. His teeth were so white (he had several gold teeth before his death). I took Daddy's death hard because I had just found him in my heart, and now he was gone. I looked at him and asked, "Why, Daddy, why?"

He said, "Sandra, I tried so hard. I just gave up. That's all. I just gave up." That gave me a peace of mind because although I never told Mom, I blamed her for his death.

I was going to tell Mom how I felt, but the urging from my sister Gail prevailed as she said, "Please, don't tell Mom. You will kill her!" I never wanted to kill Mom, but my pain moved swiftly as I blamed her for not having Daddy's high blood pressure medicine refilled. My thoughts were that she could have made sure Daddy had his high blood pressure meds simply because she worked at a hospital. That was my pain and displaced anger talking. Daddy could have picked up his own meds; he chose not to, I guess. Thank God I never told Mom what I was feeling, but she sensed that I pulled away from her. After Daddy told me in a dream that he just gave up, I ran to my mom in my heart and never let her go ever again. That short time that I pulled away from Mom was too long for me. Thank you, God, for an awakening spirit.

While in Warrant Officer School, I told this story about Daddy to my friend Mac; he was deeply moved by my testimony. He told me he was estranged from his dad, and for many years, he wanted to see him but did not want to anger or hurt his mom if he did. After hearing my story, this gave him courage to reconnect with his dad. I felt the joy as he spoke about his dad. He asked if he could share my testimony, of which I was pleased to know that it could help someone else harboring animosity, bitterness, hatred, unforgiveness, or anything that hinders them from a closer walk with God. Prayerfully, they will let go and let God have his way in their hearts.

Message from God: Prophetess Kathy

Fort Polk, LA
2001

Kathy grew up in our house as an adolescent when their house burned down until after her graduation from high school. Just like any family, we grew up and went our separate ways. I enlisted in the military, and Kathy stayed home and found work with a well-known company. I was midway through my military career when I received a phone call from her. Overjoyed, we chatted for quite a while. The atmosphere was set, but the message was not received for what was to come next.

Kathy said, "I am calling to tell you that God has charged you with keeping the family together."

"What? How dare you! I have not heard from you in years, and you are going to call me to tell me something like this? Everybody is grown! How am I supposed to be in charge of grown people? What the heck am I supposed to do? You got some nerve calling me with this mess." I was angry. She didn't say a word through my ranting. She let me rant and rave until I was done talking.

In a soft voice, she said, "I'm just calling you to tell you what God said." This was a lot to unpack on a person. It was a lot especially someone who had no idea what to do with what was said. This stirred my spirit, and I did not know how to shake it.

Shortly thereafter, I went to Sunday service as I often did. The pastor spoke on Ezekiel 3:17–21: "A watchman appointed over the land." I gasped as I listened intently to the sermon, absorbing every word as a sponge. *Lord, are you saying I am the watchman, and my family is the land?* The way I understood this scripture as preached is when God gives the watchman a message to tell a person of their wrongdoings to save their lives, if the watchman does not give the message and the person dies, that person's blood will be on the watchman's hands. If, however, the watchman gives the message and the person does not listen to God's warning, if the person dies, that person is accountable for his own blood and wrongdoings.

My mission was calling me into action because my family's blood was not going to be on my hands. When God dropped in my spirit to do or say something to any of my family members because of my family's ways, I did not hesitate to let them know that what they were doing was not of God (selfishness, unforgiveness, backbiting, gossip, adultery, etc.). I still do this practice when necessary, which extends beyond family members. Whenever I spoke to them, I reminded them that what they do with what was said is what they do with it, but their blood is not going to be on my hands.

There were other incidents of concern, but what grieved my spirit for years was regarding our mom. My older sister was Mom's caregiver and would give me updates on Mom. Several brothers lived not less than thirty to forty minutes away. They would not call to check on Mom, and they would not come home to see Mom. God dropped in my spirit to have a family meeting. I spoke to one of my brothers about this, and he told me to be careful on which voice

I listen to because it might not be of God but the devil's (something to that effect). I was a little confused because what could be wrong about discussing issues as it relates to Mom and her well-being and what they were doing or not doing? Still, I did not have a family meeting.

Years later, I still had an unrest as my sister told me more of her attempts to get assistance from our brothers regarding Mom, but to no avail. Her phone calls to our brothers were ignored and not returned. I called my brothers individually and told them the perception they gave about the lack of care for Mom's well-being. I reminded one brother that he said Mom was going to be his first lady, which is how he treated Mom until he remarried. After marriage, he rarely called Mom, and even though they went to the same church, he would not say hello to Mom there or stop by her house after church, of which he had to pass to get to his house. When my sister had to work in catering, she asked him to keep Mom until her shift was over but got back a little late. I asked how dare he let Mom leave his house at 2:00 a.m. instead of letting her spend the night and be picked up in the late morning instead? I asked if he could not watch Mom overnight while our sister worked. I told him she said he called her at work and asked when she was coming for Mom. He listened and did not say anything about the information that I heard about how Mom was treated. To my understanding, nothing much changed.

I told another brother that he is a minister, and God might have a word through him for Mom, but she would not get the message because he would not call her or take her to his house and to their church to receive the spoken words. I reminded him from what I was told that he would not call nor visit Mom. I told him he let his mother-in-law stay in his house for over a year, which is his right, but he couldn't get his mom for a weekend. His children did not bond with Mom because he did not bring them around to meet her, and they lived that close to her. He married and stopped growing with the extended family (us). He rarely visited or attended family get-togethers, particularly for the holidays. His memories were that of when we were children and his "remember when" stories were stuck in childhood. He said something to the effect of who was he to say anything if I had a message for him. To my understanding, nothing much changed.

Our oldest brother, Vernon, was a DJ and drove limousines. He lived his life battling sickle-cell disease and went through too many crises to count, but he refused to live a defeated life. He marveled over how Mom never left his side, made a way for him when he had to get to the hospital without a car, and how Mom massaged his back to try to ease the pain. He went on and on about how grateful he is to have Mom in his life. Why, then, would he not go and check on Mom when he moved out on his own? As I told him, what was said about his visits/calls or lack thereof, he justified that with work.

"You have to understand. I am a disc jockey, and I drive limousines," he said.

I asked, "So you can't find time to see your mom?" I reminded him of those things he had told me about what Mom means to him and how he loved her and appreciated her. I responded, "Is this how you show her appreciation? She is getting older, so show her now."

Somewhere in the conversation, I must have rattled his nerves because his voice went high as he angrily said, "I can't promise you that I have time to go stop by to see Mom!"

I responded, "Don't you dare think you are doing me a favor for going to check on *your* mom! She is *your* mom, and I am not looking for a promise from you on when or if you should see *your* mom."

He said that when he goes to get his haircut, he would stop by to see Mom.

"Mom has to wait for your haircut for you to visit her?" I continued, "For each haircut, you had to pass Mom's house, and you couldn't stop by to say hello?" As the floodgate of my truth opened, I let it pour.

He did not say much after that, but his actions spoke louder than his words. Vernon's wife would call me from time to time and say, "I don't know what you said to Vernon, but he took your Mom some fruits. He had lunch with Mom. He stayed with Mom. He took your Mom some flowers." For years, Vernon gave Mom homage and doted over her. Then Vernon started telling me how he would call our other brothers and give them a piece of his mind because our sister told him she called them for whatever reason about Mom, and they did not get back with her. When Vernon spoke with one brother, that brother said she didn't say it was an emergency. Vernon's response was "If you get a call about Mom, whether it is an emergency or not, you better call back." My sister said Vernon stopped by regularly, visited, sat, and talked with Mom until the day he died. To God be the glory!

I do not believe my brothers' actions were intentional or spiteful. It is my belief that Mom was more out of sight and out of mind. They revolved around their own immediate family and seemingly gave little reverence or attention to the extended family. Everyone is more interactive nowadays. No one can recapture a memory that they did not help create, but life goes on. We can start from the present to create lasting memories.

The good news is that my spirit is no longer stirred, and I walk daily in peace for doing what was dropped in my spirit. If anyone, whether family or not, says or does things that do not align with God's will, I speak up and tell them of "my" truth because I stand firmly that people's blood are not going to be on my hands. I do not profess that I am free from sin, but I sure repent often, asking God for forgiveness of my sins, known and unknown; and I am receptive to correction. When God drops a word in my spirit, I convey with loving kindness, tact, and humility. I do not want anyone's blood on my hands. What they do with it is what they do with it.

CHAPTER 7

God Works in Mysterious Ways

Fort Benjamin Harrison, Indiana
March 1994

Major emergency surgery

I arrived at Fort Bragg in June 1990. The first thing on my agenda was to have a tubal ligation. I asked the military doctor to burn, tie, and cut my tubes; but the doctor refused. He said he has seen too many women who asked for that procedure and met someone, married, and wanted a reversal of their tubal ligation. I assured him that I was a single parent, and if I married again, he would have children, I would have children, and we would pool our children together to be as the Brady Bunch. As amusing as that sounded, he still refused; I was not happy. There was no doubt in my mind that I did not want any more children. The doctor opted to clip my tubes but would not burn or cut them. Two months later, I was deployed to Saudi. I was the new kid in town and did not have time to make friends before deployment, but I gained some sister/friends for a lifetime after deployment.

Fort Bragg was the best assignment of my military career. That is probably because it was the most fulfilling assignment for me. Four female soldiers asked to speak with me on the first day of my assignment at Fort Bragg. "You are going to try to come in here and make changes," they said. "It is not going to work. You are going to write us up. Pssst…write us up. No one is going to support you. We are the misfit unit, the reject unit, and no one cares."

I sat in awe as I listened to these four junior soldiers say what sounds to me as a cry for help. I was a newly promoted Staff Sergeant (SSG) and never supervised soldiers before. God blessed me with wisdom and understanding so I could be sensitive to their needs and at least make them have a sense of purpose and feel good about themselves; that technique worked.

Our section processed reassignment orders. Some of the soldiers demonstrated unprofessionalism when dealing with customers. There were fistfights, cussing out senior Non-Commissioned Officers (NCOs) or outright disrespect for them, and nothing happened. I came in with impact statements; we are going to be the professionals that we are supposed to be, and if we do not know how, we will learn to be professionals. We will treat people with courtesy and respect. Your job is a direct reflection of you, so give your best "you." We are a team, and teamwork is paramount. This is "our" house, and no one runs our house but "us."

I learned a long time ago that no one cares how much you know until they know how much you care (President Theodore Roosevelt). The soldiers began to see that someone cared and reciprocated in kind. It was not long before our section became highly motivated, so much so that soldiers from other sections were asking if they could come and work for me. We made work fun. Our section's motivation shot to an all-time high, and that reverberated throughout our workplace and during physical training (PT) sessions. The results were so compelling that it became a domino effect where other sections within the company became highly motivated. It was not long before our soldiers seemed to care and became more confident that started a positive shift in the atmosphere. The transformation could not be denied, and if I never see another transformation ever again, that one is etched in my mind and in my heart.

December 1993 was the time of my departure from Fort Bragg. That was bittersweet because I had a connection with the soldiers who I came to love dearly. The needs of the Army sent me on Temporary Duty (TDY) training en route to my new overseas assignment to Seoul, Korea. It was during that time that God kept me close and did not let go. I was in the Advanced Non-Commissioned Officer Course (ANCOC) for twelve weeks of training. Within thirty days of training, I began to experience unexplained abdominal pain that was subtle at first but grew worse daily.

I went to our Troop Medical Center (TMC), complaining about abdominal pain. The doctor said I had a urinary tract infection (UTI) and gave me Septra for ten days. The pain subsided, but after the tenth day, the pain intensified. Another visit to the TMC yielded nothing of concern for the doctor. I was asked to lie on the bed to be examined. When he pressed on my stomach, nothing happened, but when he released the pressure from my stomach, I felt that I could claw the ceiling with my fingernails and toenails and with a mighty grip. That was excruciating pain. The doctor said they did not know why I was having this pain. They checked several other things but could not identify the pain I was having at the time.

The pain pills given did not seem to work for long; it was nearing graduation from the course within a few weeks, and I was now having unbearable pain. I volunteered to go first for our end-of-course Drill and Ceremony (D&C) marching commands. I marched the platoon with various marching movements and afterward told our instructor that I had to go to the TMC.

By the time I arrived at the TMC, I was taking very small steps because each step bore excruciating pain. When I got to the doctor's office, in a weakened voice, I said, "You have got to do something. It hurts to sit down, it hurts to lie down, and it hurts to kneel down. I am in so much pain. You have to do something."

The military doctor said they would take one other test—a pregnancy test. Who would have thought? The test came back positive. I was pregnant in my tubes from January to early March. A military doctor wrote in my medical records—well, before the pregnancy test—"Ruled out pregnancy." They did not take a pregnancy test until then, so how was that ruled out? My only explanation was that my records indicated that I had a tubal ligation in 1990. It is my belief that had they not seen that, they would have taken a pregnancy test from the first or at least the second visit.

I was in a military training environment, and the nearest hospital was the Community Hospital right outside of the military installation. The military doctor called the ER doctor at the Community Hospital to tell him about my diagnosis. The civilian doctor asked how I was going to get there. The military doctor looked at me and asked if I could drive to the Community Hospital, of which I said yes. The ER doctor was not having that and yelled, "She will not drive! You will send her by ambulance," of which he did.

Upon arrival, the ER doctor said they would do a laparoscopy, a term I had not heard before, and then determine where to go from there. After the laparoscopy findings, the ER doctor pointed his finger in my face and said, "Bottom line is this, we operate and we operate now. *You do not* get a second opinion." I was wheeled in for a major emergency surgery, and I don't remember counting as they do when given anesthesia. The surgeon removed my left fallopian tube, my left ovary, and part of my right ovary.

I am a kept person. Thank you, Lord, for keeping me. If my fallopian tube had ruptured from a baby growing inside, that would have been a fatality from internal bleeding. God had work for me to do, and he kept me. God saved me, for he was not through with me yet.

Lifeline to Life
My Heart to God's

"Write, for these words are true and faithful" (Rev. 21:5).

The Army's way of life is to start with Physical Training (PT) consisting of various calisthenics for mind and body conditioning and at least a two-mile run for five days a week. Running was a struggle for me, but once I learned the techniques of running, I ran with ease. It was likely that I would participate in a 5K or 10K run and finish within the top for my age group.

In 2001, while assigned to Fort Polk, LA, something began to change. We all slow down as we age, and we no longer have the stamina and endurance that once was, but this was different. I had begun to slow down to the point that I fell out of group runs, and that did not set well with me; I just could not keep up with the group runs; something was wrong. I pushed myself harder but to no avail. The group runs were becoming too fast for me. There was a straggler patrol truck following the formation to pick up stragglers who fell out of runs; maybe it was my foolish pride, but my refusal to get on the truck demonstrated my don't-quit attitude. I never rode on the straggler patrol truck before and had no plans to ride one then; still, I lagged behind and finished my runs.

Not long thereafter, while running and doing PT on my own, I felt discomfort in my left wrist and left elbow. *Hmmm, better get that checked out* was my thought. More runs throughout the weeks, more discomfort, and finally,

I began to become a little more concerned. A visit to the Troop Medical Center (TMC) yielded nothing wrong. My electrocardiogram (EKG) was normal. Doctors found no reason to be overly concerned, and if medical professionals didn't think it was serious, neither should I. Nonetheless, I paid close attention to what my body was trying to tell me.

Many more runs, and the discomforts intensified. At first, there was no pain, but there certainly was enough discomfort to keep going back and forth to the TMC. Each time, medical professionals would send me back home with nothing to be alarmed from, but now, it caused some concern for me. The discomfort in my left wrist and left elbow when running started to become a little painful to the degree that I would put my arm in a sling using my reflector belt. Soldiers were required to wear a reflector belt around their waistline for driver's visibility and for protection of not being hit by a moving vehicle. In one of my runs, the thought that it was not safe to run with a sling hit me because if I tripped and fell, there was no way to brace myself from a fall. I began to wear the reflector belt correctly—around my waist.

More TMC visits were just as futile as before, but God showed up and showed out—thank you, Lord! It was October 17, 2002, when I had another episode that, to me, warranted attention. After our PT exercises, I ran alone when the pain in my left wrist and elbow intensified. I stopped running, and it went away. When I started running again, the pain in my left wrist and elbow returned, this time with a discomfort in my chest area. It seems that the pain was exacerbated so much that the remaining time was spent walking. Once I returned home, I decided to do some sit-ups, but the chest discomfort was not working with me. I decided to lie down, but in doing so, my chest discomfort felt worse. Heart disease was the farthest thing from my mind because I had no knowledge of heart disease in my family, and the doctors already ruled out anything wrong with normal EKGs. I sat on the side of the bed and told God I was going to shower and go back to the TMC. When I stood up, my jaws tightened, and I felt nauseous. I went to the bathroom to vomit, but nothing came up and I felt weaker. Okay, God…I will shower and go to TMC. I felt worse in that short time and relented—okay, God. I will go to the TMC before I shower, and I did.

This time, the doctor took some blood work and said the results would come back in three days. I left a message about my chest discomfort on my commander's voice mail and went home. By Friday afternoon (October 19), my commander came in to tell me he had some good news and some bad news. "The bad news," he said, "pack your bags because you are being deployed to Afghanistan." The good news, he said, was that I did not have to leave until next Friday.

From that, I told him I would not put a foot on that plane unless he gives me a lawful order. I reminded him I had left a message on his phone, telling him of my chest discomfort, which he said he had not listened to. I told him that if he gives me a lawful order for me to board that plane without being medically cleared, and if something happens, everyone and their grandmother will know about it. He reminded me that nondeployable status required a Permanent 3 (P3) profile. Otherwise, the colonel may make me deploy. When I told him not only do I not have a P3 profile, I will also not have one in a week. I reiterated that the only way I will put foot on that plane is if he gives me a lawful order, and if he deploys me without being medically cleared, and if something happens, everyone and their grandmother will know. I could see the concern on the commander's face. One thing the military frowns on is negative attention drawn from the public, but he was warned of my intent.

Look how God works: On Saturday, October 20, I received a phone call from Alex, someone I dated at Fort Bragg from 1990 to 1992. We had not spoken since before I left Fort Bragg in December 1993. He said, "Sandy, I am coming to see you at Fort Polk," and I told him I had a Permanent Change of Station (PCS) in February 2003, heading to Germany. Then I told him I had been having chest discomforts, and his tone changed to concern as he said, "Sandy, you go to that doctor and demand an MRI! Do you hear me? You demand an MRI! I will not lose you too." The urgency of his tone got my attention. An MRI never crossed my mind, but I listened intently. By Monday morning, the week of deployment, I went back to TMC and demanded an MRI. I told the doctor that if he cleared me for deployment without fully clearing me medically, if something happens, everyone and their grandmother will know. He, like the commander, showed concern and set me up for an appointment with a civilian cardiologist.

The civilian cardiologist took pictures of my heart, did a stress test, and then took more pictures of my heart. He said the bottom of my heart was not beating as aggressively as it should have been for just getting off a treadmill. He consulted with another cardiologist, and both agreed. They thought I needed a heart catheterization. I never heard the term before but left it up to the medical professionals. That night, I went to Bible study and later asked the pastor if they would pray for me because of my chest discomforts.

His response was, "Sister Hayes, I did not know he was talking about you." He had gone to a church conference the past weekend, and the bishop told him that the devil is trying to take someone out in his congregation, and it has to do with the left side of the heart. After the prayer, Shirley, a Major (Army Nurse) told me she had no idea he was talking about me.

Shirley said she worked on the third floor of the hospital. She always goes out the front door, but for some reason, she went out the back door. She had to pass the TRICARE office and a friend saw her and called her in. He wanted Shirley's opinion on whether or not to approve my getting a heart catheterization from a civilian cardiologist; no name was exchanged. "I think she is trying to get out of a deployment," her friend told her. Shirley asked for a little more information, and he gave her my vital signs. She said, "High blood pressure [BP] runs high particularly in blacks." (My pressure had spiked to 145 over triple digits, and I was almost fifty with a high BP.) She said she would approve the request for a heart catheterization, and so he did.

Satan did not stop there. On Wednesday, two days before deployment, the military Physician Assistant (PA) called and said, "Chief, the cardiologist thinks you should have a heart catheterization. Do you think you need a heart catheterization?"

I did not know what a heart catheterization was, so I put the ball back in his court. "Doctor, do *you* think I need a heart catheterization?"

There was silence, and then he said, "The cardiologist said yes, so yes, I think you should get a heart catheterization."

That afternoon, the PA called me back to say he did not feel comfortable with me having a heart catheterization and then two days later putting me on an airplane. It was about that time when I heard the Holy Spirit say, "You ain't going nowhere."

I was the only one at home. The PA explained they have to go into the main artery in the groin area and pump dye in the body to watch its flow. High altitude could cause that puncture site to rupture. The PA asked me for a name whom he could talk to about my case, and I gave him our colonel's name and number. Later, he called me back to tell me that he spoke to our colonel. He told the colonel what the cardiologists recommended and what was to follow. Then I clearly heard the Holy Spirit say again, but this time rather sternly, "I said, you ain't going nowhere." The PA said he explained to the colonel the heart catheterization procedure and the danger of being in high altitude potentially rupturing that punctured site. The PA said our colonel said, "She ain't going nowhere." I smiled because I already knew that from the Holy Spirit.

Desperate times require desperate measures, and Satan seemed to ramp up his antics because there was more to come. The PA called me back to say it would cost tens of thousands of dollars to do a heart catheterization with a civilian cardiologist, so they decided to transport me to Brook's Army Medical Center (BAMC) in San Antonio, Texas, which was two hours away. Army doctors come through BAMC for medical training. I am sure they had already reviewed my medical records, but one of the cardiologists looked at me and said, "We won't find anything wrong. You are physically fit, you are not overweight, you have none of the risk factors for heart disease, you don't smoke, you don't drink, and your cholesterol is one of the best we have ever seen."

I told him, "I am only telling you what I feel." It is only fair to say that although my blood pressure had spiked to triple digits over triple digits during that one medical visit, my BP was usually relatively low/normal.

It gets better. The cardiologist numbed around my groin area and proceeded with the heart catheterization. I watched them monitor my heart and the flow of the dye. They did not seem concerned and was rather relieved as they did not find anything of concern. One of the cardiologists turned around and said to me, "Exactly. We knew we would not find anything."

Then I asked, "Doctor, is it supposed to hurt like that?"

He asked where it was hurting, and I put my hand in the area of my chest discomfort. He said, "Well, let's take another look." He turned back around with a ghostlike face and said, "Whoa...your body just don't play fair!"

My thoughts were, *If I was one to get upset easily, this would be the time, but they are supposed to keep the patient calm.* The cardiologist said, "Just look at you. You would not see anything wrong. My thoughts were, you were not supposed to be looking at me but looking at my symptoms." He went on to say they found a left main coronary aneurysm (LMCA) three times the size it should be. He ranted some more and said, "Chief, I'm just going to be honest with you. We don't know what to do. We only see things like this in the operating room or..." Then silence. Then he said, "No one walks in and says something is wrong with this kind of diagnosis." He said they had to confer with other colleagues and get back to me because they were baffled. They put me in the hospital for a week until they made a decision. While in the hospital, a family member called crying when they heard of my diagnosis. I told him, "Get off my phone. If you can't call with an uplifted spirit, you will not call me with a downtrodden one!" They got off my phone, and I hung up. I was calm and did not need that negative energy. After the weeklong hospital stay, the cardiologist put me on medical leave for thirty days. They were still baffled.

Our colonel made an appointment for me to go to the National Institute of Health (NIH) in Bethesda, Maryland. I believe they wanted to study this rare but miraculous discovery of the aneurysm. I did go, and they ran batteries of tests. The cardiologist at BAMC gave me his name and number and asked me to keep in contact with him. I honestly think they believed I would not last as long, but thank God I am still here and well.

They were leery of surgery because the location of the aneurysm was on the curve of the heart, making this a very dangerous operation. They told me what could happen with or without the surgery. If the aneurysm gets larger on an already-weakened area, it could rupture, causing a fatality (internal bleeding). Then they could put me on medical management with medication to slow the heart rate down—metoprolol (Lopressor), calcium, baby aspirin, Zocor—stop! "If you said I had one of the best cholesterol counts you had seen, why would you give me Zocor?"

"Because," he said, "once a person is diagnosed with heart disease, they want the cholesterol count to be lower." I agreed to the medical management. I was given a P3 profile but knew that with a P3 profile, I could not relocate to Germany. What? They want me to stay at Fort Polk? That was not going to happen. I was on an overseas assignment to Germany in February 2003, and I was going. I did get a cardiologist to downgrade my P3 profile to a P2 profile, which allowed me to go to Germany, but I had to agree to get an MRI every six months to make sure the aneurysm did not get larger, of which I did agree to the terms.

Within a year of arrival at HHC, 1st Infantry Division in Wurzburg, Germany, I was slated for deployment to Afghanistan. Here we go again. I told my supervisor that I could not go because of my medical diagnosis. I could not carry a rucksack, duffel bag, or even deal with the triple-digit heat in Afghanistan; I was already given a weight restriction (no rucksacks) and certain PT exercises that I could and could not do. More importantly, I had to keep my stress levels down.

My supervisor was adamant. "Chief, I need you with me."

"That is not going to happen, ma'am. I cannot deploy. Technically, I could deploy with a P2 profile, of which I had with the downgrade from a P3, but I believe a cardiologist, knowing my condition, would not sign off on me deploying." They pushed the issue for me to deploy, the surgeon general got involved, and I could not deploy.

One would think the worst was over, but when the devil was trying to stop me from my destiny, the fight continued. After over twenty-one years of military service, I retired on September 30, 2005. I was staying with my daughter and her husband in Owings Mill, Maryland, for several months after retirement. In December 2005, I found a local cardiologist and told her of my diagnosis. She said they had to operate. I did not appreciate that and let her know that, because she had not seen the disc from my diagnosis, but she was already determined to operate. She calmed me down, took the disc, and conferred with her colleagues. Around December 24, 2005, I was told they had to operate because the aneurysm was larger. God is so good to me.

I was a contractor at the time with the United States Army Force Management Support Agency (USAFMSA). Shortly before surgery, I received a phone call. I will never forget that angelic voice from TRICARE, although her name escapes me.

"Chief Hayes," she said, "are you aware that you will be paying over $50,000 for this surgery?"

"Why?" I asked. "I am retired and have a network cardiologist."

"Yes," she said, but the hospital where the surgery will be done is not in the network" (something to that effect). She said so softly and sweetly, "I can't let this happen. I just can't let this happen." Then she said she would call me back. The next day, she called and said in her angelic voice, "Chief Hayes, it's okay now. I had to talk to my supervisor. You are cleared for surgery—TRICARE pays." Thank you, Lord!

Satan continued to try to touch and stop me, but I imagined God saying, "Touch not my anointed one" (Ps. 105:15). The night before my scheduled surgery, my oldest sister, a retired nurse, called to talk to me. She said, "I know you must be anxious."

I said, "I most certainly am not."

She said, "Well, that's not normal."

In my mind, I am about to undergo a serious surgery and did not need anything to compound that with worry. I had been praying for peace, and I focused on that. If I was going to worry, I should not pray, and if I was going to pray, I should not worry. I chose not to worry. I trust God, and that is whom I conferred with.

On January 6, 2006, approximately ninety-eight days after military retirement, I was scheduled for open-heart surgery. My birthday is January 4. The day of the surgery, I looked up toward heaven and said, "Well, Lord, either you are saying that this is the last birthday I will see, or you are saying that I would see more birthdays." Either way, I was not afraid. Thank God I am still here.

The surgeon explained what the surgery entailed. He said they would give me a pencil and a notepad after surgery because I would not be able to talk. I would have tubes in my mouth and drainage tubes from my stomach. He asked if I had any questions for him.

"Yes," I joyfully said. "Are you a praying man?"

Taken aback, the surgeon said, "Yes, I pray before all of my surgeries."

I replied rather jubilantly, "Then let's do this!"

I told my daughter the first thing I wanted to hear when I woke up was Shekinah Glory Ministry's song, "Yes." My daughter, two sisters, and an adopted little sister from the military, Jannette, waited for my surgery to be over. I met Jannette in Stuttgart, Germany in 1987. We became sisters at heart. Jannette do not have biological sisters, and I became her big sister. She said if her sister was having surgery, she was going to be there, and she came. She is a gem, a keeper. I love her dearly.

I was taken into surgery for a double bypass. While in the recovery room, I saw about three nurses looking puzzled at the monitor with the leads attached to my body. No one paid attention to me, and I did not have my notepad and pencil. I hit my thigh to get someone's attention. The male nurse looked at me, and I motioned with my finger that I needed to write; he asked if I needed to write, and I nodded my head, yes. He looked back at the monitor, still with a puzzled look on his face. I hit my thigh again, and he looked back at me; I spelled with my index finger on my thigh: "swollen neck." It felt like my neck was swollen.

He said out loud, "Swollen neck."

A female nurse said, "Ma'am, there's nothing wrong with your neck. I need you to be calm."

I was calm.

No one moved to get my notepad and pencil. I hit my thigh once again and spelled "neck swollen," and the male nurse repeated what I spelled out. A female nurse said, sounding angry, "Ma'am, there is nothing wrong with your neck! I need you to remain calm."

I suppose my body was sending signals via the attached leads to the monitor that they didn't understand. I began to pray. *Lord, how can I let them know my neck has so much pressure that it feels swollen?* The pressure was on the right side of my neck where the surgeon cut; for whatever reason, I do not know. Anyhow, the next thing I heard was frightening as a female nurse said, "Oh, Lord, she's losing all of that blood. She's losing all of that blood!" And they rolled me onto my left side.

I said, *Lord, I just had open-heart surgery and they rolled me over on my left side.* I must have passed out because that is all I remembered.

They rushed me back into surgery for another open-heart surgery and had to drain blood to find out where the bleeding was coming from to stop it. This time in the recovery room, as I was coming to from the anesthesia, a male nurse was talking to someone else and said, "Whoever stitched up her neck the first time botched it up." I assumed whoever stitched the side of my neck previously stitched it too tight, and the pressure from within burst through the stitches, hence too much blood loss. I had to get a blood transfusion.

This time, while stabilized and in the recovery room, when I opened my eyes, my daughter, sisters, and Jannette were standing at the foot of my bed. I did not hear Shekinah Glory's song "Yes" as requested, but the first words I heard were my sister Jan's voice as she looked from one side of the room to the other. In amazement, she gasped and said, "Oh my gosh, Sondra. You're glowing! You look like you have a room full of angels all around you!"

I smiled knowingly. Yes, indeed I did.

Once I was released to go home, I stayed with my daughter. I had to blow to raise a ball within the tube several times a day, which helped kept my lungs clear. I had to conduct certain exercises like stretching my arms out wide and closing to prevent large keloids. I was also assigned a home nurse visits to check on my progress. As I began to gain my strength, the nurse told me I needed to start walking.

I asked, "How far should I walk?"

She said to walk a mile. The next day, armed with my pedometer, I set out for a one-mile walk. The next day, the nurse asked if I walked, which I responded with "Yes."

She then asked how far I walked. My response was "I walked two miles." Her eyes widened, and her voice pitch elevated as she said, "You walked two miles?"

While looking at her and a bit confused, I said, "You told me to walk a mile. I had to get back, so that was also a mile. Did I do something wrong?"

"No," she said. "You did everything right. There are so many people who have had heart surgeries and are afraid to move. They become couch potatoes."

She said, "You did everything right." I smiled, for I was not afraid. I was not thinking about dying; I thought about living.

Every angle that Satan tried to stop me, God blocked it. God provided other avenues of escape for me from the hands of the enemy; I call those avenues of escape my rams in the bush. I heard from Alex on October 19, 2002, and prior to that, it was about ten years since we last spoke from the days at Fort Bragg. To present, I have not heard from Alex again; it's as if he had that message only for me to demand an MRI. I truly believe that God used Alex as a vessel because, out of nowhere, he called me, I believe, to convey that message; we have not spoken since that time. God has his shield of protection all around me, and I trust him.

My first cousin and spiritual advisor Nita laughed as she said, "You don't get sick often, but when you do, you do it big."

Satan tried to take me out too many times, but even Satan cannot stop my destiny or the plans God has for me. My belief is that I am sitting in the palm of God's hands, and he showed me that nothing can pluck me out. I believe that wholeheartedly.

Sergeant First Class (SFC) Johnson, Retention NCO

MacDill AFB, Tampa, Florida
Spring 1999

"Do unto others what you would have them do unto you" (Matt 7:12).

My first duty assignment as a newly assigned Warrant Officer 1 (WO1) was to HHC, 3rd Infantry Division, Fort Stewart, Georgia, with duty at MacDill AFB. We were a team of about twelve soldiers assigned to the Personnel Service Support Team (PSST) that provided multifunctional personnel services operations to four-star commands and other tenant units.

My Non-Commissioned Officer-in-Charge (NCOIC), SSG Brown, was a female Staff Sergeant (SSG). She was selected for Drill Sergeant (DS) duty and needed to get more physically conditioned for the rigid training needed to train soldiers. In other words, she had to be a strong runner as one of the requirements to meet vigorous training; she was not a strong runner. My Retention NCO, SFC Johnson, assured me that she would get her in top condition before her report date for DS school.

Report date came for her attendance at DS school and SSG Brown was indeed ready for the arduous training that awaited her. My retention NCO told me that our soon-to-be DS promised to keep her informed of her DS training progression. Most interestingly, SFC Johnson asked her family to keep our soldier in their prayers as she goes through DS training. A few weeks passed, and there was no direct news of SSG Brown's DS progression. That angered SFC Johnson to the point that she said SSG Brown promised she would keep her informed, and she did not. She said she was praying for her and asked her family to pray for her. Now, she will stop praying for SSG Brown and tell her family to stop praying for her.

With a grieved spirit for her comments and without hesitation, I told SFC Johnson that this was not a Christlike behavior, and that she was wrong for doing that because SSG Brown's fiancé kept her abreast of her DS progression. That was no comfort for SFC Johnson as she said angrily that she didn't say we would get updates through her fiancé. "SSG Brown said *she* would let me know how she was doing." Updates from her fiancé were totally unacceptable to her. She said once again she will no longer pray for SSG Brown and will tell her family to stop praying for her.

I cautioned her that God does not like ugly; her actions were ugly, and she should continue praying. She was not hearing that, and I finally conceded, still trying to convince her to keep praying. While raising my hands toward heaven, I said, "Fine, SFC Johnson, that is between you and God." God must have convicted her heart because immediately, she started flailing her arms in the air, yelling, Oh, Chief! Why did you do that to me? I have to find a closet. I have to find a closet. I have to go and pray!" I'm looking at her as if she lost her mind. She left my office rambling about finding a closet and needing to pray.

She came back into my office with her arms flailing in the air, saying, "I have to find a closet! I have to pray! I have to pray! I just stood there watching her and not knowing what to do. The next day, we had a Physical Training (PT) test with three events (pushups, sit-ups, and a two-mile run). We must score high enough on each event from a chart that identifies them based on gender and age; a failed PT test would result in additional after-duty training in preparation to retake another PT test a few months later.

I had already passed each event on my PT test and cheered soldiers as they crossed the finish line for the two-mile run. SFC Johnson, a strong runner, completed her run with about a minute to spare; she had cramped at the halfway point and barely passed the run event. As soon as she crossed the finish line, she came straight to me and said, "See what you did, Chief! My assumption was she referred to the previous day when I tried to convince her to keep praying for SSG Brown. She had displaced anger, for I did nothing except surrender her to God.

A few days later, my cousin, Prophetess Kathy, called to say hello; and I told her about the entire previous conversation between SFC Johnson and me about continuing prayer for SSG Brown. I told her there was nothing that I said that seemed to make a difference in SFC Johnson's mind; therefore, I told her that was between her and God. Prophetess Kathy laughed and asked, "Don't you know what just happened?" This, I had no idea of. She said, "When you tried to fix it, nothing happened, but when you turned it over to Jesus, he fixed it."

Scripture reminds us that we should pray without ceasing, pray one for the other, and bear one another's burdens and so fulfill the law of Christ (Gal. 6:2; 1 Thess. 5:17). Scripture also reminds us that we were made sorry, but that "ye sorrowed to repentance; for ye were made sorry after a godly manner, that ye might receive damage by us in nothing" (2 Cor. 7:9). This scripture has meaning to me, which it is not because of anything that I said convicted SFC Johnson's heart, but it was because of God.

Mom

July 2000

> Write, for these words are true and faithful. (Rev. 21:5)

Sometimes we need to stop long enough to be still and listen. This is my belief to avoid any regrets and wishing you listened to that "something told me to" voice. That something, a still, sweet voice, could be the Spirit of the Lord talking to us, which may sometimes be brushed aside, dismissed, or overlooked. Mom told me something years ago that left me with fond memories. Thank God for obedience.

While on military leave and visiting Mom, I was reading *The Divine Revelation of Hell.* What was interesting was the author's description of people in hell: arms flailing between bars, wailing in agony, and crying out in pain. The awe of the book compelled me to tell Mom about that excerpt from my reading. Much to my surprise, Mom said that when she was a young girl, she had a dream that she was walking on coals of fire behind Jesus in the pits of hell. People were reaching their arms through bars, like in a jail, trying to touch Jesus and crying out to him, but they could not touch Jesus nor her. Jesus and Mom kept walking, and Jesus did not look to his left or his right; he just kept walking. Mom walked behind him. She said it was so hot in the pits of hell. The Lord's words and Mom's dream was more than enough to keep me aligned with walking closely with Jesus.

Shortly thereafter, Mom said, "Sandra, if something should happen to me…" A lead-on statement like that made me feel uncomfortable that Mom was about to say something that I did not want to hear. Death is inevitable, but it is still not a welcomed conversation. I prayed, "Lord, please let the phone ring. Please let the phone ring," hoping that Mom would forget about what she was about to say. The phone rang, and I thanked God. God must be a humorous god, for I looked up toward heaven, smiled, and said, "Okay, Lord, I didn't ask you to let it be the right number." It was the wrong number.

Mom continued, "Sandra, I know all of my children love me as best they know how, but if something should happen to me, I want you to hold your head up and hold it high. You have nothing to feel bad about because you give me my flowers *every day*," she said. "I know you will miss me, but you will be all right." Now, I know how Mom felt. My children love me as best they know how, but I will not be able to say to them what Mom said to me. Children are our pride and joy, but they grow up and find their own way in life much like we did; they may have other interests that do not include *us*. Some pull away from family and may find their way back or not, but nonetheless, we love and keep them uplifted in prayer. We know we are connected by bloodlines and by the love in our hearts, but we have to let them go. We taught them, nurtured them, and watched them grow, so we should trust our teachings and let them go live their lives. I taught my children to be self-sufficient and independent, and they are both. For that, I find pleasure and great joy. They were taught strong family values, so now they will have to find a way to employ that love more in their lives with me, if it is important to them. Either way, I love them very much and call them my prodigal son and daughter.

No matter where my military obligations took me, and no matter what I was doing, Mom was at the forefront of my mind and my heart; I made quality time for her. After all, we only get one mom (biologically), and we do not get to choose; God knows what he is doing. It is my belief that God prepared me to look to him and not to people; otherwise, I could get hurt. I can only imagine the hurt and pain families go through because their children do not dote over them or sometimes do not even keep in contact. People change, but God is steadfast; he does not change. He is the same today, tomorrow, and forevermore. I choose to chase after him and not after grown children. For that awakening, I am eternally grateful to God.

Years later, Mom was diagnosed with dementia, but what she poured into me stayed with me. As my sister Sylvia still describes me, I was so busy keeping my head up Mama's dress that I had no time to explore places beyond Mom and our small community; I was a mama's girl and left home after I married, which Mom lived about forty minutes away. It is my belief that God prepared me for Mom's death.

I kept a notepad and pencil on my bed to journal dreams or whatever was poured into my spirit in the wee hours of the morning. My alarm clock was set on weekdays at 4:30 a.m.; my workday started at 6:00 a.m. The alarm went off, and I knelt to pray as I often did. In the midst of my prayer, I heard the Holy Spirit say, "Write."

I looked up toward heaven and asked, "Write what, Lord?"

With absolutely no idea what to write, I turned on the light; retrieved my notepad and pencil; and while still on my knees, armed with writing materials, I did not have to wait long before words poured into my spirit. I penciled those words on two sheets of paper.

The first thing I did, once settled at work, was scan those two sheets to my computer and email them to my sister Sylvia. "Good morning," I said. "I make no excuses for writing about Mom in the past tense. I was saying my prayers, and in the midst of my prayers, I heard the Holy Spirit say, 'Write.' I looked up and asked, 'Write what, Lord?' Everything written was about Mom, how members in church and in the community perceived her, what people were saying about her good will, her kind heart, her character, her spirit of humility, her personality, everything."

Six months later, Mom succumbed to the progressive dementia. Debbie, Sylvia, and I were in Mom's room, singing her favorite gospel songs because it was evident that Mom would not last through the night. Jan was on the Amtrak outbound from New York to South Carolina to be with Mom; she did not make it home in time. Debbie and Sylvia were engrossed in the songs but they were not looking at Mom while I watched her intently; around midnight, she took her last breath.

"She's gone," I said. Now all attention was on our sweet, precious, and loving mom, as she would not exhale another breath. Our sister-in-law, Veronica, sent me an email of a dream that she had of Mom the night she died. I call it the bride and the bridegroom.

While making plans for her homegoing service, I told God that he poured those words in my spirit six months prior, and he has got to give me the strength to say them. With calm, poise, voice projection, and inflection, I spoke those same words that God poured into my spirit with ease. Within the six-month period of God telling me to write until Mom's death, other people would tell me what Mom meant to them. Who would have known that six months later, Mom would be gone? Mom's homegoing service was as grand as the life she lived. I miss Mom, my Queen Bee, but I am all right. It has been over eleven years since Mom went home, and I am still standing strong on her words that keep me grounded. Immovable, I stand on the words, give me my flowers now while I can see them, smell them, and feel them; that is what I did for Mom, and that is what I do for anyone whose path intersects with mine. Amen and Amen!

Andy

Bob Evans Restaurant
Summer 2017

Andy, a scraggly white man, was homeless. He was unkempt, dirty, and smelled. His teeth looked as if they needed a good brushing. Bob Evans was where I spent every Saturday morning for their piping-hot, delicious breakfast. Customer service was very welcoming and receptive. Not far from the entrance door of the restaurant is where Andy stood.

Each Saturday, I would walk past him as his eyes looked for a connection, which I avoided for a little while. Faithfully, he stood there every Saturday morning, glared in my direction, and I did not press toward making eye contact. This particular Saturday, my heart was convicted, and I asked him if he had eaten. His reply was no. "Come on in," I said. "Sit at the counter and get something to eat." I told May, a beautiful-spirited host, to give him what he wanted to eat, let him order something to go, and give me the check. This became a Saturday ritual. Most of the time, I would give Andy $20 to put in his pocket before he left.

Andy became a regular patron of Bob Evans at least for breakfast on Saturday mornings, as I made sure he ate breakfast, took a meal with him, and had spending money for later. One Saturday morning, when my niece Kenish, who was studying for her graduate degree at Howard University, visited me, I took her to Bob Evans for breakfast and motioned Andy to come in, sit at the counter, and eat. May, an excellent host, took very good care of him as usual and gave me the check as Kenish and I sat in a booth talking. I told Kenish what I did each week for Andy, yet I always let him eat alone. That grieved my spirit.

The next week, I sat at the counter with Andy, and we ate breakfast together. We introduced ourselves and talked briefly. I asked what his story was, and he said, "You really don't want to know." He had some rough years. He talked a little about mostly living in the woods. I didn't want him to think I was prying, and we mostly ate with occasional conversation.

Finally, Andy said, "Sandra, I don't want you to think that I am taking advantage of you."

I responded, "Stop! You did not ask me for anything. Whatever is going on is between you and God. God's Words say we are to feed the hungry, clothe the naked, visit those in jail, and whatever I can do to align with his words, I will do that. Andy, you do not owe me an explanation." We smiled at each other and kept eating. He ordered his take-out meal, I gave him some money for later, he thanked me, and he left. Shortly before the pandemic, Andy stopped showing up at Bob Evans, but I think about him often. I pray that all is well. Matthew 25:35–40 speaks holistically about God's commandment to help those in need. I help others as best I can in the name of Jesus.

Renewed

New Orleans
October 2017

Marilyn

Many people struggle from battles within. The need to feel accepted, loved, needed, wanted, embraced, included, and forgiven can weigh heavily on us. Such is the case with my longtime friend and sister at heart, Marilyn. We may pray and ask God for certain things, yet we do not know when our prayers would be answered and only at the appointed time deemed by God. I ask God to use me so I pray that God would "speak to me and through me that whomever I am talking to, he knows it is something they need to hear; all of him and none of me."

Marilyn, her husband, sister, and brother-in-law came to visit me a few years ago for her birthday celebration. We toured DC and saw so many beautiful sights. Throughout the week, Marilyn would reach out to her sister for affection, love, a kind word, or even a hug. Her sister did not seem as receptive to embrace and express love to Marilyn. While observing Marilyn continually reaching out to her sister, her sister would seemingly cringe at Marilyn's approach toward her. Then I would hear, "What? What do you want now?"

Marilyn would ask, "Could we just take a picture together?" or "I just want a hug."

Her sister's body language and rolling of her eyes made it clear that she did not want a hug or to take a picture but hurriedly stopped long enough to take pictures.

By midweek, Marilyn sat on my bed, and we talked about varied topics in general that led into the week's observations. My spirit was grieved for what I'd seen so far with Marilyn looking for familial love and not getting that kind of love returned. Over two decades ago, in the early nineties, Marilyn, my supervisor at the time, spoke to me of the dysfunction in her family, which did not seem to change decades later. Marilyn served in the Army for over twenty years, and her family seemingly ousted her out of their lives, not merely because of her military service. It should be a blessing that Marilyn is independent and financially stable. Anyhow, even then, Marilyn longed for but was void of her family's love and affection. I listened intently and felt the pain as she spoke; she had a little girl's spirit, needing belongingness and acceptance.

While reflecting on the lack of her sister's interaction that was still far from Marilyn's touch, I said, "You know she is only tolerating you."

Marilyn said, "What?"

"Your sister," I said, "it seems she is trying to get through this week with you. She's tolerating you." I continued, "So far, every angle that you have tried to reach her has been shut down by her moving away from your embrace, responding harshly, or just keeping her distance from you."

Marilyn, a reverend, looked at me with sad eyes and said, "Sandy, I've always known that but never heard anyone say that before." Know that even people in the ministry have trials, tests, and tribulations. They struggle with some of the same things we struggle with who are not in ministry.

I reminded Marilyn that she is trying to fix their family's relationship, but she should give them to God come what may and let God have his way in their lives, for she needs to work on herself. My reassurance that her family loves her in their own way did not lift her spirit. It's now time to take action for Marilyn to feel loved. I grabbed her hands and said, "Stand up!"

As she stood with a downtrodden spirit, I looked her in the eyes and said, "Marilyn, no one is going to love you like you would love yourself—self-love and self-care. Love *you* for a change." I told her that she has tried for decades to fit in and fix things with her family, but that was beyond her control; she should turn them and it over to God.

I ushered her over to the mirror in my bedroom. With a stern voice, I said, "Tell that person looking back at you in the mirror that you love her!"

She whispered, "I love you."

I said, "I don't believe that! Do you honestly believe that? Tell that person in the mirror that you love her!"

She said a little above a whisper, "I love you."

"Say it again!"

She said, "I love you."

"Now, say it like you really mean it!"

She said with conviction, "I love you! I love you!"

Compassionately, I told her, "Every time you pass by any mirror, look into that mirror and tell that person looking back at you that you love her, but say it like you mean it." I looked her in the eyes and told her, "Marilyn, when you find your peace and when you find your joy, no one will be able to take that from you. The only way they will take your peace and your joy is if you give it to them. You already know what it is like to have discord, unrest, and a longing for love, so when you find peace and joy within, you won't let anyone take them from you because you will know what it feels like with and without them. Be concerned about how you feel about yourself and not what they feel toward you. Let God do his work with them."

By December 2018, I attended another sister/friend's fiftieth birthday celebration in Louisiana and stayed with Marilyn for the week. Marilyn sat on the bed, and with her sweet innocent voice, she said, "Sandy, I didn't get the chance to thank you."

I asked, "Thank me for what?"

She said, "For saving my life."

Stunned, I said, "Come again?"

She replied, "For saving my life." She said that before I had that talk with her, she was thinking about suicide, heart attacks, and strokes. She said, "You saved my life. I love the person I am now," and that she surrendered her family to God and left them there.

My spirit rejoiced as I said, "To God be the glory. Thank you, Lord!" Marilyn is about two years older than me; I could have said anything to her that could have pushed her over the edge such as "You are still talking about the same thing you spoken off over a decade ago. You need to grow up." I could have said anything, but I chose to speak to her in love about love and God's love. Thank you, Lord, for setting a watch before my mouth and for keeping the door of my lips (Ps. 141:3). We know that the enemy comes to steal, kill, and destroy (John 10:10). Let no one steal your joy, kill your spirit, or destroy you. Marilyn is now a bundle of joy with a natural high; her spirit is renewed, revived, and reenergized. She looks and sounds great. Glory! Hallelujah!

CHAPTER 8

The Art of Forgiveness

New Orleans
February 2001

My girlfriend Marilyn said to me, "Sandy, you can't come to Louisiana and not go to the Mardi Gras." I was in the military and assigned to Fort Polk, LA; my son had just started college. Of course, we took Marilyn up on her offer to go to the Mardi Gras. Once we got to her house, I asked if she was going with me, but she said, "If you have seen one Mardi Gras, you have seen them all." She did not go. She did, however, send me with her teenage son who was about my son's age and two other teenage brothers she fostered.

On February 25, 2001, I was no longer thrilled about the Mardi Gras experience because if I still decided to go, I had to go with teenagers. I chose to follow through with it because I wanted my son to get the experience; I certainly was not going to hang out with male teenagers. My son did not know any of the teenagers, for this was the first time they met. Once we got to the Mardi Gras, her son positioned me on the main street where I watched the parade and people who threw beads at us from the parade. I told them I would be right here; the teenagers took off and ended up on Bourbon Street. My son followed because he surely did not know his way around.

Later, as I stood right where they left me, one of the foster teens ran up to me yelling, "Ms. Hayes, they arrested your son!"

My heart pounded with the news I just heard. "What?"

"They arrested your son!"

"Why?"

"I don't know," he said. "He was just standing there and they arrested him."

I ran to the spot where he took me, but my son was nowhere to be found. I called his cell phone, and he answered. "Where are you?"

"I don't know," he said. "They put me in the back of a truck where I later found out was a Paddy Wagon." They held him there until the Paddy Wagon was full, and off to jail they would go.

I called Marilyn and told her what happened. She told me there was nothing I could do until morning. They would not start booking people until then. She said, "This was Louisiana's biggest revenue maker, and charges are often trumped up, especially for people who came from out of town." She called her son and told him he had better get me back home safely, and he did. I, of course, could not sleep and started calling the police station early in the morning. I was told he would be in a cell, and booking did not start until 9:00 a.m. Later, Marilyn took me to post bail.

They charged my son with lewd and lascivious behavior and resisting arrest. The bailiff (I think that is who he was) asked my son if he did this. His reply was *no*. The bailiff told him to plead not guilty, and they would give him a court date for August. He also told my son that when he comes back to court in August, he should plead not guilty and ask for an expungement of his records. Shortly thereafter, I asked my son what happened. He said he was just standing there, smiling, and a policeman came up to him and asked how old he was, and he said eighteen. The police told him to get off Bourbon Street, and he asked why. The police grabbed his arm, and he told the policeman to take his hand off him and snatched his arm away. They wrestled him to the ground, handcuffed him, and took him away.

There was no question in my mind that my son did not do those things he was charged with, which in small terms was flashing body parts. I am not saying this just because he is my son, but because my son, a very quiet person, would not flash his body parts. He wore clothes much too big because of a term I called cover; he camouflaged his tall and skinny body frame every day with clothes that were not fitting but are even too large for his body size. He would have been out of character if there were any truth to the charges. I understood the smallest infraction of resisting arrest when he jerked his arm away. Anyhow, we went back to Fort Polk and continued with our daily life until we had to come back to New Orleans for court in August.

On August 23, 2001, I took my son back to court. When the judge asked him how he pleads, my son said,

"Not guilty." The judge threw out the lewd and lascivious behavior and gave my son a fine for resisting arrest. He also expunged my son's records. We went back to Fort Polk, relieved that this was not worse. That night, I called Marilyn to tell her the outcome of the court's proceedings.

It was then that she said she, "Sandy, I have a confession to make." She knew in February that my son did not do those things he was charged with. He said when her family came home, she told them they had better tell her the truth because she knew it was one of them. The truth was that one of the foster teens was responsible for that arrest, so to speak. The foster teen told her that my son was just standing with his arms folded and smiling. There were so many people at the Mardi Gras. One of her foster teens, a short guy, would stick his hands up women's dresses and scoot away. When the females turned around, they saw my son standing there with his arms folded, smiling, and figured he was the one who was doing that and reported him.

She continued with her confession that she could not tell me the truth because of the foster teenagers. She would have been in trouble with the state because the foster teens were not supposed to be out of her care, and they were at the Mardi Gras without her. I could not believe that she knew since February and allowed my son to take a false rap, a fall, to protect her from losing the foster teens. That is how I summed it up. She apologized, of course. I realized that she did not have to confess, but she did. I wondered if the outcome was more severe if she would have confessed, but there was no way I will ever know. I don't think she realized that those charges on my son's records could have had long-lasting effects with a negative impact. Thank God my son's life was not negatively impacted because of those charges.

I forgave Marilyn for what she put my son through. We are still very close sister/friends to this day. Sometimes, we share stories and experiences with our circle of friends. When I told other friends about this experience, the response was often "She would not be my friend. She jeopardized your son and his clean start in life." I would hear, "How could you trust her again?" The responses varied. Forgiveness is often hard to do, but I have found that others go on living their lives with no thought of how the person they wronged is coping with the wrongdoing. We seem to nurture the hurt and pain, and they have no idea what we hold on to, so I say, let it go.

Finally, I am reminded of Matthew 18:21–22 when Peter asked the Lord, "How many times should I forgive my brother and sister who sins against me? Seven times? Jesus saith unto him, I say not unto thee, until seven times: but, until seventy times seven." I choose to forgive. What she did is between her and God. I will not give fuel to something that could hinder me from going forward and keeping my peace. I forgive her, and I love her as a sister.

It's Not Your Fault
#MeToo

Fort Polk, LA
February 2002

While assigned to Ft. Polk, LA, I had a Command Sergeant Major (CSM) friend named Ron who was stationed in Germany. Ron called me one day to tell me he had a friend coming to be the Installation Command Sergeant Major (CSM). "Take care of him please."

"Sure! A friend of Ron is a friend of mine! Tell him to come to the Personnel Services Battalion [PSB] when he needs me."

As fate would have it, I was the Staff Duty Officer (SDO) for an overnight shift of security inspections among other required duties. It was late, and I was hungry. I was munching on various nut combos and raisins mixed in a sandwich bag. While on Staff Duty, our Battalion Sergeant Major introduced the inbound Installation Command Sergeant Major to me.

"Soooo you are Chief Hayes," he said, smiling.

"CSM Frazier! Ron told me about you. If you need anything, let me know. I am at the PSB."

CSM Frazier made the ultimate mistake of helping himself to my snack "without asking" by sticking his hand in my snack bag, and I went off: "As long as you know me, don't you *ever* help yourself to nothing that belongs to me without asking. Not now, not ever!"

We were off to a bad start, but I was assured that we now have an understanding; all is well. I will never forget that smirk on his face as he smiled; it seems I became a challenge to him, but I did not know what was coming next.

While working in my office late one evening, CSM Frazier called, asking why I was still in the office. I said, Bible study starts soon, and I did not want to go home so I'm working until it's time to go to Bible study."

"Swing by the office before you go please."

"For what?"

"Just swing by for a few minutes please."

After much badgering, I said, "Fine, for a little while."

There would be no mistaking now about being off to a bad start. He was not someone I wanted to be around. That was not a good visit, and I never wanted to be in his presence again. He offered me wine; invited himself to my house for beer, tea, water, anything; and that was not going to happen. I got up to leave as soon as he started making advances, and he blocked the doorway. I reminded him that we were in the staff building with the general's SDO, and if he did not let me out, I would scream so loud that the SDO would come running. He let me out. I ran to my car, and before I could put the key in the ignition, he was at my door. He said, "I just wanted to see what kind of car you were driving. You have tinted windows and a garage [houses on the installation have garages]. Let me come to your house." I pulled off.

I stayed away from him, but we went to the same church where he said some inappropriate things that during the meet and greet, coming to me and asking me for a hug, talking about how good I looked, and the likes. Each Sunday, I steered away from him. I would not let him near me long enough to have a conversation. He started showing up unannounced at my office. People really do not need to announce themselves to come to the PSB, but as the Installation CSM, there is a certain protocol to follow, so for him, everyone should have been informed to give him the respect rightfully due as the Installation CSM. He would call me on my office phone throughout the day and once at 3:00 a.m. For that, I gave him some choice words and told him to lose my number. Voice messages from him at the office were deleted with no return call.

To show how he usurped his authority or maybe it was his arrogance, I was in my office giving my newly arrived Staff Sergeant (SSG) my standards-and-expectations briefing when CSM Frazier barged in my office.

"Chief Hayes, I keep calling you, and you won't return my calls and that pisses me off."

The SSG stood up to leave, and I told him to sit down; I stood up. "Sergeant Major, get the hell out of my office, and don't ever come in here like that again."

He said, "And you call yourself a Christian."

It's funny how my faith was attacked for not falling for his shenanigans. I told him, "I call myself a servant of the Lord. Now, get out and please don't come back." I told SSG to never leave my office unless I excuse him, which he said he thought that was about religion. CSM Frazier's visits to see me had begun to draw attention, and I did not like that.

Upon my return from an absence one day, my first-line supervisor told me that CSM Frazier came to see me. "What's your point, sir?" I was annoyed that he did that. He said he was letting me know that he came to see me. I told him he is free to come to the PSB any time, which he responded, "He came to see you."

"Thank you for the message, sir," and I went back to work. CSM Frazier was working my nerves, but I did not have to be around him nor work with him so I could get pass with avoidance. The only time I would see him outside of the intermittent office visits was at church. Everything up to this point were just words, so I really did not hone in on him much since we had little interaction.

Christmas season came fast. I was sitting at my desk when the phone rang, and I answered. It was CSM Frazier. He said he just called to wish my family and me a Merry Christmas, which I returned the Christmas greetings. Then he said, "Chief, this is for you…muuaaahh," sending a kiss. He asked, "Well?"

"Well, what?" I asked.

"Aren't you going to kiss me back? I will do no such thing. You will get well-wishers like everyone else."

He said, "You would either give me a kiss, or I'll take it." I hung up the phone and continued working. My computer was against the wall with the entrance to my office on my left. I was helping a customer using my computer, and the phone receiver on my left shoulder for balance while I looked up information for the customer. From my peripheral vision, I saw a shadow come from my left, and by the time I looked to my right, CSM Frazier bent over and kissed me on my lips. I told the customer I'd call him back. He said, "I told you if you didn't kiss me back, I would take it," and he left just that fast.

The game changer came months later when the both of us went on a Temporary Duty (TDY) assignment at the same time with the same return date. We did not work together, and our TDY was in different places (don't know if he had a connecting flight; I did not), but we were on the same plane at the same time. It was a small airport with those small passenger planes. We were sitting directly across from each other and were being civil to each other. I knew nothing could go wrong on an airplane. Oh, was I wrong.

I sat next to him just to say hello. He said, "Chief, I was just thinking about you." He said he can have anyone at his fingertips, and he chooses me. He said, "You won't stop until I make you a private again." I was not worried about him demoting me to a private, but before I could slide over to my seat, he grabbed my hand, thrust, and held it to his groin area, and said, "See what you do to me?"

I said, "If you don't let my hand go, I will scream, and someone on this plane knows you are the Installation CSM." He let me go.

My son was waiting for me at the baggage area. Once the plane landed, I walked toward my son, forgetting that CSM Frazier was on the plane. He ran behind me, asking to take me home. I told him. "My son is picking me up, so leave me alone. As I got closer to my son, who came to meet me, CSM Frazier ran up to him, shook his hand, and introduced himself. I told him to get the hell away from my son and leave me alone. He smiled and walked away.

I called Ron in Germany and told him, "I don't know what you told your friend but call him off." I told him the things he was doing or saying and that I was too embarrassed to tell him what happened on the plane. I said, "I felt violated and ashamed. Call him off!"

Ron said a few sentences: "I can only imagine." He added, "I have something that might help." With Ron's concern for me, he sent me a newspaper clipping of CSM Frazier's face in the *Stars and Stripes* newspaper as Top NCO in Kosovo under investigation for allegations.

What I disliked about the Army is that it seems, for senior leaders, that if you mess up, you move up. They moved him from Germany with allegations to be the Installation CSM at Fort Polk; imagine that! He continued to do more of the same. I am grateful for a friend like Ron who was concerned about my well-being to inform me of his friend's wrongdoings. I pray God will continually bless Ron abundantly for his kindness and concern. Thank God for people like Ron.

I called my dear friend George, retired Sergeant Major (SGM), who was working at the Defense Logistics Agency (DLA) in Virginia and told him what CSM Frazier was doing and saying to me to include what happened on the plane and the threat of making me a private. I told George I was not concerned about him making me a private again. I also told him about the newspaper clipping that Ron sent to me. George reminded me that CSM Frazier worked directly for the general. He could make up and tell the general something about me that was not true. He urged me to send CSM Frazier an email from my office and BCC myself to my personal email, which I did. George's vast knowledge of military procedures at the senior-enlisted level helped to seal the evidence of the email that was used in the investigation. George was a God-sent; thank you, Lord.

Much to my surprise, after TDY, I had missed our newly arrived Lieutenant Colonel's (LTC) command philosophy. While summoned to her office, I thought I was going for her command philosophy but walked into the middle of a full-fledged investigation. I was caught totally off guard because she was the appointed investigating officer, and my name was in a black book that outlined CSM Frazier's every stop.

From what I was told later from a reliable source, CSM Frazier invited his driver and wife for Thanksgiving dinner. Afterward, he gave them a tour of his house. When he took them to the garage, he sent his driver in the house to retrieve a book of some sort. When the driver came back, it was the wrong book, and his driver was sent back into the house to get the right book. Upon his return the second time, his wife said she wanted to go home now. He took her home, and she told him CSM Frazier tried to kiss her. The driver got his gun and went back to the house. His wife answered the door, and he told her he came to shoot CSM Frazier. She said he was not there, which he threatened him by saying that he is going to the general first thing in the morning with his open-door policy and with his black book, and he did. That started the investigation flowing. His driver took notes of everywhere CSM Frazier went—some using a military vehicle for nonmilitary reasons.

After LTC Robins briefly told me why I was there, I had to sign a sworn statement, and the questioning began. I broke down and cried uncontrollably. She wanted to know why I was crying, which I said, "I was so angry with me because I stopped him from bothering me but had no idea he was messing with other women. I should have known that if he tried that with me, the likelihood that he would have tried with someone else was possible. If I had just filed a report, maybe that would have started some kind of investigation. I did not file a report." Riddled with guilt again, I was so very angry with *myself* for not reporting him simply because of two reasons: he was Ron's friend, and there were not enough people of color in such a high position. I did not want to be the reason he was relieved of duty. I did not stop to think that *he* not *me* would be the reason for his fall; he was doing that to "himself"—doing things that could cause him to be relieved of duty. I was so broken in heart and spirit, not for him but for me.

LTC Robins told me my name was in a black book, "Get with Chief Hayes at the PSB," and she needed to know the nature of that visit. I told her he would show up unannounced at the PSB, kissed me unexpectedly once on the lips, and called me, but I was not interested in nonwork relations, among other things that he did. Then I told LTC Robins about the email that I sent to CSM Frazier, asking him to leave me alone. She said they pulled every email out of the Directorate of Information Management (DOIM) system, pertaining to CSM Frazier's inbox and sent files, and there was nothing there to support what I was saying. Between tears, I told her I also sent a BCC to my personal email at home. She told me to go home, bring the email back the next day, and she would tell my commander she released me for the rest of the day. LTC Robins said, "Chief, I promise you, he will never do this to another person."

The email simply stated, "Your office calls are unwelcomed. Your phone calls and advances are not welcomed. Leave me alone or I will have to report you. If you can't come to the PSB on professional business, do not come." I would hate to see a repeat of what happened in Germany; he knew that I knew something and left me alone; I was happy. After I sent him the email, CSM Frazier still taunted me by coming to the PSB, sticking his head in the door, smiling/waving, and saying, "Hi, Chief, I'm here on professional business" and kept going, but he left me alone.

Shortly after the Army's 15-6 investigation started, I was diagnosed with a left main coronary aneurysm (LMCA), which was three times the size it should have been. Some things take a little time to come to terms with. I had to process my diagnosis and could not let what CSM Frazier did coupled with what I had to deal with medically cause unnecessary stress to my already-compromised heart. Immediate leader's mission was in keeping me calm, so I don't put extra pressure on the already weakened area of my heart. With my return from Brooks Army Medical Center (BAMC) in San Antonio, Texas, I was met with a voice mail that I had to report to Criminal Investigation Division (CID) to be questioned by an agent.

Once the investigation started, CSM Frazier knew he was in serious trouble. He called me and sounded like a man with a broken spirit. He sincerely apologized for what he did, said he needed help and was going to get help, and asked me to forgive him. I forgave him, knowing I did not ever have to deal with him again.

To make matters worse, that night, I sought counsel from our pastor. The first lady answered the phone and wanted to know the nature of the call. I told her I wanted to discuss CSM Frazier. She said the pastor knows about that and began to tell me that CSM Frazier's wife had a dream about me. I don't remember the details of what she said about the dream, but it had to do with her husband and me. Whether it was a dream or a concern from observation of her husband's advances towards me in church, I do not know. That probably explained why one Sunday after church service, CSM Frazier's wife came to me and asked to pray for me. I don't turn down prayer, but when she held my hands and started praying. Lord, this is a mighty woman of God, and I ask that you rebuke the devil out of her right now in the name of Jesus. *What?* I thought. *Why is she praying like that for me? I haven't done anything!*

Nonetheless, the pastor returned my call. Pastor said that CSM Frazier told him all about what he did to me. He said, "CSM Frazier told me he asked you to forgive him, and God wants us to forgive." He asked me, "Did you forgive him?"

I said, "Yes, I forgave him, but I had to see CID the next day."

Pastor said, "CSM Frazier realized he needed help and is getting help."

"What are you asking me to do?"

"I am not asking you to lie," he said, "but if they do not ask, you do not have to volunteer information."

"What?" I asked. "You want me to lie or downplay what happened? I am going to tell them everything that happened. He was a pastor and a First Sergeant (1SG) of a company. It did not matter that he was the pastor, and truth should prevail."

Pastor made this worse for me, not better. I felt victimized all over again. I was highly upset, and I yelled, "I have to see CID tomorrow!" I hung up to slow my heart rate down.

I was still somewhat upset when I went to the CID office. They started a line of questioning, and I could feel my heart rate increase. I said in a stern voice, "What do you want from me? You have my sworn statement! I was just diagnosed with a left main coronary aneurysm and have not processed that yet. They wanted to keep me calm and rightfully so for a weakened area of the heart." They did not continue with their line of questioning and let me go. There was more to tell the CID agent with the in-between of my experiences with CSM Frazier, but the timing was all wrong, considering my diagnosis.

After CID's completed investigation, he was relieved of duties immediately and retired. I told Niecey what happened with the pastor and CID. She told me that pastor's wife and CSM Frazier's wife are first cousins. To me, this explained the pastor's response to our discussion. I realized that his pastoral or First Sergeant obligations were not a priority; protecting his family's honor was of most importance. Maybe he did not care enough to think that he victimized me all over again. That hurt.

Then I had an epiphany. Why worry about something beyond my control? If I could have controlled what happened or my diagnosis, it would not have happened. Thank you, Lord, for that revelation. I have a new attitude. I went to work the next day, and with a more cheerful and uplifted spirit, I said jubilantly, "Good morning."

My commander walked up to me and said, "Chief, I don't understand you. You come in here saying good morning like nothing happened. If I had a diagnosis like yours, I would be pulling my hair out."

I chuckled and said, "Then what, sir? You would still have what you have but with no hair." I refused to live a defeated life. Sometimes we have to change how we process things to move forward. Additionally, sometimes, we have to encourage ourselves.

I was broken because I stopped CSM Frazier from bothering me but did not give a second thought that he was "possibly" doing that to others; how could I have been so selfish or insensitive? These are some thoughts that victims wrestle with from the traumatic experience. We should hold our heads up with assurance that we are not responsible for someone else's actions; they are. Put ownership where it belongs. I realize that if we knew then what we know now, we may have done things differently, but we don't know what we don't know. We cannot turn back the hands of time and only try to go forward with a new perspective on living our best life. That is easier said than done, but for me, I will keep trying no matter how long it takes. Each day of small progressive steps in the right direction will eventually become a giant leap. I will not give my power away. There are others experiencing more traumatic experiences than this, but help is readily available just for you and me. Seek help and try not to do this alone because we are not alone. We are stronger together.

About a decade later, George told me that the pastor, as a first sergeant, had an obligation to report this, and he did not. As I relived those events with a mental health doctor and blaming myself, she told me I did do something by telling pastor; she said that I was suffering from survivor's guilt. I got him to leave me alone but could not stop what he was doing to others. I found some comfort in what she said that he could have assaulted others before he tried with me, so there was nothing I could have done. As a named victim of his assault, I was able to request a copy of the CID report.

A Look in the Mirror

HHC, 1st Infantry Division
Wurzburg, Germany, 2004

Our division, HHC, 1st Infantry Division (1ID), deployed to Afghanistan; and I was the Rear Detachment Adjutant General (AG) Chief, Warrant Officer 3 (CW3). We had a small team who remained in the rear (home station) to process all of the division's multifunctional personnel services while the division deployed down range and to assist the deployed soldiers of anything they needed from the rear.

One day, shortly after beginning our workday, one of my female soldiers (her name escapes me), closed my door to have a heart-to-heart talk. She was highly upset because of the actions from her first cousin, which she previously and affectionately called her little brother. Her first cousin grew up in their home and was referred to as their younger brother. My soldier and her cousin/brother were closer in age and very close in relationship, like siblings.

As her cousin/brother grew into his teenage years, he became quite troublesome. The most recent episode landed him in jail; the family was distraught. My soldier was very angry because her mom raised him as her own child, and she did not appreciate him taking her mom through all of those unnecessary changes from his misbehavior.

Her other siblings wrote to him while he was in jail, but she could not forgive him and, therefore, chose not to write to him. She said her cousin/brother would constantly ask other family members to ask her to please write to him because the two of them were the closest, but she could not do that because of her unforgiving spirit. While attentively listening to her, I kept saying within my heart, "Help me, Holy Spirit," because I wanted the Holy Spirit to tell me how to respond. She was adamant that she could not and would not write to him because she just could not find it in her heart to forgive him for the things he put her mom through for so many years; she was angry.

Finally, God ministered to my heart. She was asked three questions: "Did you ever do anything wrong that you asked God for forgiveness?" She said yes. "Do you think that God forgave you for the wrong that you did?" She said yes. Lastly, I asked, "If you believe God forgave you for your wrong, how is it that you cannot forgive your brother for his wrongdoings?" She began to cry, and I just let her release until she felt better.

The next morning, after arriving at my office and before I was able to put my bag down to start the workday, that same female soldier came into my office. She had a jubilant spirit; and with great delight, she said, "Chief, I wrote my brother! The joy that was within was almost too much to contain." She said she was so happy, and she left to get her workday started.

Sometimes, we have to look into the mirror of our hearts because we often see the mote (speck) in someone else's eyes but cannot see the beam (log) in ours (Matt. 7:3–5). Furthermore, it seems as if there was a weight lifted off her as she forgave her cousin/brother as God forgave her and allowed herself to love without judgment.

CHAPTER 9

For I Am God, and There Is None Else

Eisha

February 1986

My first military assignment after basic training was HHC, 1st Infantry Division (1ID), Fort Riley, Kansas. It was there where I met a few of my lifelong military friends. During that time, one young lady befriended me. I felt like she was a younger sister to me. Our jobs were the same: Administrative Specialist. We got along very well. She had a two-year-old daughter who lived with her grandmother.

It was not long before she met a young man that she fell in love with; he had recently separated from the military. They dated for several months and were to be wed in December. This was quite disturbing for me because I could see déjà vu all over again. She met her soon-to-be husband in September and was supposed to be wed in December of the same year, 1985; I was her maid of honor. Throughout those three long months, I pleaded with her to wait, get to know him better, and then make plans to marry. That plea fell on deaf ears.

Her story was almost like my story. I met my ex-husband in September 1980 and married him in December 1980. I had a five-year-old daughter at that time. That marriage lasted two years, but what happened within those two years I would not want anyone else to experience. Prior to our marriage, it did not seem to bother him that I had a five-year-old daughter, when in actuality, it did. He was in the Navy at the time that we met, and I was offered a job at DuPont but was indecisive on whether to take the job or not. He encouraged me to take the job, telling me he knew about his knowledge about DuPont from his hometown in North Carolina; I took the job. As I reflect on those times, it seems like I served his purpose, for he was soon to be discharged from the Navy unbeknownst to me until it happened in February 1981, about two months after we married.

I told my friend my story so she could think about her marriage proposal some more before December, hoping that she would delay her plans to marry. My ex-husband was so mean to my daughter and to me; I intervened, of course, on my daughter's behalf but could do little about that when I was at work. I told my girlfriend that I would get home after my second shift (4:00 p.m. to 12:00 a.m.) and get home shortly after midnight from work. My five-year-old would be home alone, asleep on the couch. When asked where my then-husband was, she would reply, "He left right after you did and never came back." I ended up paying a babysitter for my daughter's safety. There was a time when my daughter was eating jelly beans shortly before bedtime. After watching TV, we went upstairs, and I told my husband I had to check her mouth because she was eating jelly beans.

He said, "Don't worry. She'll just choke and…"

I looked at him and said, "And what!?"

He looked at me and walked away.

My hope was that she would see the severity of knowing this man only for a short period of time and wait to be wed. I pleaded with her to let him find a job first and then marry. My life was an open book, in the hopes that she would pull from it. My story did not mean it had to be her story, but we were treading along the same path. My daughter wanted him to accept her, he did not seem to care. She was my flower girl, and she stood in front while taking wedding pictures, crying silently. My little girl cried through most of our wedding ceremony.

My daughter played with a little girl next door who had long, beautiful hair. My ex-husband would compliment the little girl so much that when my daughter, wanting his attention, would say, "Daddy," he would respond, "Don't call me daddy! I am not your daddy!"

I can only imagine what she felt because she heard compliments given to her friend and could not get a compliment herself from the man who lived with her. She wanted his acceptance so badly, and that was not happening. My daughter played independently/alone on the floor, and my ex-husband would say he could not stand to share me with anyone. I told him, "Husbands come and husbands go, but nothing on God's green earth will change the fact that that's my child!" I continued, "If I ever have to make a choice, you are gone." I had to make a choice, and I chose my daughter. He is a changed man today and remorseful; I forgive him.

I told my friend I chose to veer off course by filing for a divorce. I felt my job was to tell her that she was headed for a brick wall, and she could choose to veer off course or hit that brick wall with her eyes wide open. I had to pour out to her because it was as if there was an uncontrollable train wreck waiting to happen, and she was the only one who could stop it. Before marriage, she would say that her fiancé and daughter would go to the movies, the buffalo pen, or get some ice cream. I looked at her fiancé standing there, saying absolutely nothing, and looked back at her with teary eyes and said loud enough so he could hear, "Please don't do this! Please do not push your daughter on him. Get to know him first. He is standing right here and never opened his mouth about what they will be doing together! Please do not push your daughter on him! Please don't do this!"

The wedding date was rapidly approaching. The day she married, I pleaded and actually cried, asking her not to do this; the marriage was a go.

My girlfriend did not hide her intentions. Shortly thereafter, she began to talk about going to get her daughter, of which I shed more tears, followed by more pleas, asking her to get to know him for herself before she went to get her daughter. She married in December 1985 and got her daughter in February 1986 to live with them. Her daughter turned three years old in March and was given a birthday party. I still have the picture of my son sitting next to her at her birthday party. Before the month was out, that precious little girl was dead. She was killed at the hands of her stepfather. I took her death hard, and it weighed on me heavily. I can still see me at church, broken and crying uncontrollably, where a circle of women dressed in white with hands interlocked, forming a circle around me; I was brokenhearted. I would not be so descriptive with the gory details of her death, but if I had to describe it, she was as a ragdoll in his grips. I pulled the newspaper clipping from my safe that I kept of her murder but chose not to disclose the nature of her brutal beating.

I was enraged now and played the blame game for myself. I should have seen signs, I should have said something with the one thing that I did see, which was her foot/ankle bandaged when he brought her to the office. He had her on his hip with her bandaged ankle/foot.

"What happened to my child?" I asked him. He said he was ironing, and she was playing on the floor and tripped over the cord; the hot water from the iron burned her foot. I turned to her mom and asked her, "Is he beating my child?"

"No," she said.

"How do you know? You are at work."

"Because," she said, "I asked her if Daddy hits her, and she said *no*.

"What do you expect her to say!" I yelled. "She could be a scared little girl!"

Her husband was standing right there as I said that, and he never said a word about my statement. I did not report to the First Sergeant (1SG) what I had seen. I blamed myself for over a decade for not saying anything about her bandaged ankle/foot. I was now on a mission. No other child under my watchful eyes would die of such a death as hers. I vowed that I would become a judge, jury, and executioner. That statement played in my heart and wholeheartedly in my life for over a decade.

It was not until August 2000 when I was assigned to Fort Polk, LA, did I have a little relief, so to speak. I was in church talking with one of the deacons after a service and told him the story of that precious little girl's death. I spoke with conviction and authority, "No other child under my watchful eyes will have a demise like that." I cried uncontrollably.

He said, "You have to let that go. There was nothing you could do about that." I found no comfort in what he said. "You have carried this too long," he said. "You have to let it go." I heard him clearly but wondered, *How? How do I let it go?* The pain was as if it happened yesterday, I am still "broken" but stand on my convictions of being a judge, jury, and executioner to keep any child under my watchful eyes safe.

Court-Appointed Special Advocate (CASA) Volunteer Eden

Alexandria, Virginia
April 2010

I find pleasure in giving back to the community, and what better way than through volunteering. I was retired from the military at this time but kept volunteering as I did while in the military. This time, I chose to become a Court Appointed Special Advocate (CASA) where I was sworn in by a judge to be an advocate in the best interest of the child. As a CASA volunteer, we were given a case and had to interact with the parent(s) and child and anyone who came in contact with the child(ren). If the judge ordered parenting classes for the parents, I had to talk with the facilitators to see if parent(s) engaged in the parenting discussions. I would have to go to daycare, foster care, play areas, at home, or in public where the child interacted with other children and give a written report of each session to help the judge make an informed decision. This was short of social work but helped with their overloaded cases.

When asked why I wanted to be a CASA volunteer, I told my story of what happened at Fort Riley and the death of that sweet little girl in 1986. I was passionate about taking good care of the children. They listened intently and, because of my passion, decided to give me a case that was befitting the situation of the family coupled with what happened in 1986. They felt I would come in with attentive details for the case to protect the child; after all, they knew about my vow of being a judge, jury, and executioner to keep children safe. I was told that the case should not take longer than six months, but this case took well over a year.

I had to go on my first visit as a shadow with Darlene, the caseworker, for training. Darlene would review my report for clarification if needed before forwarding the report to the judge. She told me to take a toy for the child to win her friendship. I took a handheld Dora toy, and it was hard. Eden's mom had to sign release papers for me to interact with her and her child in any setting. Eden had seen so much violence in her young life between her mom and dad who were living together, and it showed. Eden wanted her mom's attention; her mom was busy reading paperwork for the required signature, and she told Eden to wait. Eden's little face turned to anger; she brought her arm back, and we heard a loud cracking sound—POW! Eden took that hard toy and smacked her mom on her jawbone. Darlene and I looked at each other in shock. Eden was only two and a half years old, but she was big for her age.

Eden was an angry child, but she was also fearless. While watching her play in the play area at the mall, if one of the children angered her, she would push them down and take a stance with balled fists over him or her, as if saying, "What are you going to do?" I would look at her mom, who would jump in, of course, to stop Eden. The child's size (bigger or smaller) did not seem to matter to Eden. If she was angry, it showed. At their apartment, I interacted more intimately with Eden. I would get on the floor with her, play with her, laugh with her; and she loved it. We were building a rapport; I had won her trust. Each time she saw me on a visit, wherever that visit took place, she would smile and yell, "Ms. Hayes, run to me and give me a great big hug." I beamed with joy.

One day, I chose to see how she interacted with other children in the after-school care. By that time, Eden was three years old. Eden had some toy horses that she lined up on the windowsill, one behind the other, when a little girl came by and swiped the horses off the windowsill and onto the floor. My heart pounded. *Oh dear.* I waited for Eden's anger to break through, but I was pleasantly surprised. Eden looked up and asked the little girl, "Why did you do that?"

Eden collected the little horses and began the display once again. My spirit rejoiced as I fought back tears. I said while smiling, "She's blossoming right before my eyes." I was very proud of how Eden handled that situation. This truly was a breakthrough for her. Oh, happy day! This was a joy to behold. Eden and I had many more months having fun, laughing, playing, and growing closer. I did not realize I was getting too close; I was all in for this precious child who had a beautiful spirit.

Additionally, I had to interact with her dad in settings with and without Eden on allowable visitations. There was a restraining order in place, so he could no longer live with them in the apartment. We talked extensively about court requirements, feelings about the case, his feelings in general, Eden, etc. At the end of each session, I asked, "Shelton, what do you want the courts to know?"

"They think I am crazy," he would say. "I know what they are trying to do. They want to take my child."

I took notes and put them in the report. The last time I spoke with him was in April 2010. I asked the same question, but there was something different about what and how he said what was said. "Shelton, what do you want the courts to know?"

"Tell them they should be happy now."

"What?"

"Tell them they should be happy now."

It was an early April Sunday morning, and I went to the 8:00 a.m. service as I usually do and would be back home at nine thirty for the most part. The adjoining townhouses to my left and right were mostly void of little children. I arrived promptly at nine thirty back home after church, backed my Altima into my parking space, and locked my car door. There was no one in sight, as is most Sundays after I get home from church; there was nothing unusual about that. I walked up the steps, unlocked the door to my townhouse, and turned around to lock my storm door. I paused.

To my surprise, standing behind my car was a little girl that emitted a beautiful/familiar spirit; well, it felt good seeing her. I was puzzled, though. I looked around to see if there was an adult nearby, thinking, *Why is this child here alone? Someone had to be nearby.* But I found no one. The little girl stood silently while looking at me; she did not sway to the left or right. She just stood, looking at me. She was smiling, and I smiled, but I was puzzled. I looked around again for an adult, but no one was there. I figured, surely, they were nearby, so I locked my storm door and took one last look at the little girl before I closed and locked my door. She stood there, looking back at me and smiling. Before I could close my door fully, she was no longer there—vanished.

That same night at 10:30 p.m., I was watching TV when Darlene called.

"Hold on, Darlene, if you are calling me this late, I will need to take notes." I ran to get a notebook and a pencil. "Okay, I'm ready."

She said, "Sandra, I did not want you to hear about this on the news."

"Hear what?"

"Eden is dead."

I couldn't talk. I heard Darlene call my name, but I couldn't say anything. It was as if the room was spinning, and the air was sucked out of me. My head felt as if it was reeling.

"Sandra!" Darlene yelled.

I broke down in tears. She told me some of what happened. Shelton got into the apartment complex, pushed his way into the apartment, cut Seble's throat (Eden's mom) from ear to ear, and then he cut Eden's throat from ear to ear. After what seemed like forever and I calmed down, it hit me. "What time did this happen, Darlene?"

"Nine thirty this morning," she said. I knew then that the familiar spirit Eden came to see me one last time.

God…what? Why? I was confused; think, think, think. Then I remembered. For over two decades, I tried to keep my vow; no other child under my watchful eyes would die such a death; I had become a judge, jury, and executioner. I cried out, "God! Was I playing God and did not know that? Please forgive me. I am so sorry." I realized my emotions decades ago got the best of me; I was not God, and I was not knowingly trying to be God. I never professed to be God but had acted in such a manner when it came to children. My convictions were so strong from her death in 1986 that I did not stop to think until Eden's death that maybe, just maybe, unbeknown to me, I might have been playing God, and I could not protect the children like *only* God can (Isa. 46:9). My heart hurts; the pain lingers.

I asked my neighbors to be on the lookout for unusual cars and told them my story. Shelton threw the bloody knife in the hedge outside of the apartment, fled the scene, disappeared; and the police had no idea where he was. He eventually hit America's most wanted list, and they found him in New York. Shelton said Eden was glad to see him but did not know what was coming next. He said if he could not have his child, no one would.

Over the following weeks, CASA reps reached out to me, but I had shut down and did not answer their calls. The night Darlene told me of Eden's death was the last time I spoke to her or anyone from the CASA office. I blamed them for nothing. I had a meltdown, and I just could not do it anymore. When I chose to volunteer again, it was at the United Services Organization (USO) giving back to the military community. Maybe I just played it safe. I still think about Darlene from time to time; she was so nice. A few years ago, I went to the CASA office to face my giants and tried to get in, but the door was locked, and I walked away and never looked back. I would love to say hello to Darlene, but I have no idea where she is.

This story is the hardest story I ever had to tell, and my heart still hurts from these two tragedies. I lost my mom, my dad, and my brother; but those losses still do not compare to what I feel when I talk about those two precious three-year-old little girls whose lives were cut too short. The pain is new, especially when I hear of children's neglect, abuse, or abandonment anywhere. Since retirement and still blaming myself, I sought help. The hurt and pain runs deep. "I should have reported him" was my biggest cry. Counselors asked, what was I supposed to report? I did not see anything except her bandaged foot. Albeit true, I did not try to submit a report, but I am better now. I have seen mental health doctors and a psychotherapist over the years. Another avenue to help military personnel and veterans are veteran centers.

Veteran centers are there to help active military members and veterans suffering from post-traumatic stress disorder (PTSD); military sexual trauma (MST); anxiety; depression; or abuse (physical, alcohol, drugs, etc.). Readjustment counselors teach us to look within and identify triggers. We learn how to heal ourselves. Veteran centers promote self-love and self-care even when we don't love ourselves. We learn coping skills to help with unexpected triggers at any time. Support groups empower each other. We heal, grow, cope, and gain renewed strength; these are lifesavers. I implore military personnel to find a veteran center near them so they can get help; they do not have to go through this alone. There are crisis hotlines in every state for anyone. I urge you to use the resources readily available to you, even if it is not affiliated with the military.

In 1987, when the pastor told me that God has work for me to do, I wondered how I would know what he wanted me to do. I didn't want to miss his calling, thereby asking God to make me an attentive listener while letting me know when he is saying something to me. "Ask and it shall be given you, seek and you shall find; knock and it shall be opened unto you" (Matt. 7:7).

Years later, when Mitch asked if I ever stopped to think why God allowed "me" to experience these events, I did not know why. The seed was planted that day in my mind and in my heart, for I never forgot his question. I still did not know why until now. "For the vision is yet, the appointed time but at the end, it shall speak and not lie. Though it tarry, wait for it; because it will surely come, it will not tarry" (Hab. 2:3).

If someone were to ask me again, do you ever stop to think about why God allowed you to have these experiences? I would probably respond with yes. For a time such as this, the experiences became testimonies about God and how good he is. It is about the many ways that God speaks to and through us. It is about obedience in what he wants us to do. It is a story about tragedy, restoration, valleys, ups and downs, forgiveness, peace, joy, salvation, healing, and deliverance.

"A reflection would see the anger, bitterness, unforgiveness, hatred, pain, and the likes but if a man, therefore, purge himself from these, he shall be a vessel unto honor, sanctified, and meet for the master's use, and prepared unto every good work" (2 Tim. 2:21). God had work for me to do; he had to work on me so he could use me. I would say my walk has been a spiritual discovery and spiritual fulfillment as I continue to grow in Christ more and more.

I asked God to help me with whatever my plea was, and I asked him to bless me with a receptive heart to receive that which he was about to show me. Sometimes we ask God for things but are not ready for what he will show us. My receptive heart allowed me to accept that which he poured into me, even those things I did not want to see or know, and I was able to deal with and accept them. I was receptive of what God showed me. I asked God to lead me, and I would follow; he led. I realized that God has been working in and through me for decades; that is clear now.

I asked God to bless and anoint me with a spirit of forgiveness, and I learned to forgive. Forgiveness is sometimes the hardest thing to do, but God commands us to forgive, and for those walking in Christ, we have to continually fight that unforgiving spirit. We may not get second chances to make a wrong right, but we can ask God to forgive us of any wrongdoings and don't forget to forgive ourselves. Too many emotions are shown particularly at homegoing services because a loved one held on to strife, contentions, disagreements, or unforgiveness and will never get the chance to say, "I'm sorry" or "Please forgive me" or even make a wrong right.

I forgave anyone who may have wronged me. I asked God to forgive me if I wronged someone, and I work diligently to forgive myself and let it go. I do not want to nurture and feed pain, anguish, and anything that takes me out of my element of peace with God. When something takes root in our hearts, we have to pluck it up from the root so it won't grow; do not feed the pain, hurt, or disappointment. Reminders of the uncomfortable situations at hand may stay alive in our thoughts and heart, but I hone in on 2 Corinthians 10:5, "Casting down imaginations and every high thing that exalt itself against the knowledge of God, and bringing into captivity every thought to the obedience of Christ." I place those ill thoughts captive and under arrest because it hindered me from going forward. There is a lesson in everything that we do; learn the lesson and grow from it. I try to go to a happy place in my mind and remind myself of positive thinking.

God instructs us on what to think on, so when negative thoughts try to creep into my heart and into my mind. I go to Philippians 4:8. Think on these things: "Whatsoever things are true, whatsoever things are honest, whatsoever things are just, whatsoever things are pure, whatsoever things are lovely, whatsoever things are of good report; if there be any virtue, and if there be any praise, think on these things." Anything contrary to what he instructs us is out of his will. This helps me to restore positivity and keep my joy and peace. Additionally, this keeps me grounded in his words.

Through the experiences while in my valleys, God equipped me for the battles to come. I gained strength, patience, peace, obedience, and an "I trust you" spirit; I faith-walked and became steadfast as I allowed him to guide and direct my path. With a new attitude and plenty of gratitude, I ask God for a fresh anointing every day. Some of my family members say I'm the strongest woman they know. I didn't just get strong; I had to go through some things, but I don't look like what I have been through. My strength came from "life" and my struggles while I was in my valley. Sometimes he has to take us through some things, but when we walk with him, we will come out better and stronger. I ask him to make me a fisher of men; will you trust him? If so, draw near to him. Diligently seek his face and learn from him. Everything that we do is a choice.

It is often said that is just the way I am, but that is the way we choose to be. Make a choice to be a better you and grow more in Christ.

I choose to be obedient unto God as he instructs us to be. I choose to forgive. When I forgive myself, the enemy has no leverage to convict my heart with the same thing that I may be trying to resolve. I choose to trust God through my valleys or struggles, through hard times and good times. We have not because we ask not. I choose to ask, trust, and believe for my season of harvest in God's time. I choose to ask for a spirit of discernment to recognize and listen attentively to God's voice. I choose to avail myself to help others.

Why did God allow me to have these experiences? To show me the error of my ways, to cleanse and purge me from anything that is not of him, to heal and deliver me as a testament of who he is and what he can do, and to raise awareness in *you*. Hopefully, you will gain awareness of God at work in *your* life. This revelation is not merely for me but also for you. Sometimes we need sweet reminders of what God can and will do if we just ask, trust, and believe him. We often want quick responses because of our dire situation in what the natural eyes see. God, on the other hand, knows that this process, as uncomfortable as it may be for us, is necessary for our growth, for what he has in store for us and for the expected end for us—for the vision is yet the appointed time. God knows when that appointed time is, our season of harvest.

As I reflect on my life's journey, I know without a shadow of a doubt that all things, indeed, were and am working together for my good (Rom. 8:28). I couldn't see it as I was going through the experiences/valleys, but I undeniably see it now. I asked God to give me patience to long endure, and patience was granted. God has been my ram in the bush for many avenues of escape. My heart rejoices, for we are blessed and highly favored, chosen by God to be here. God breathed the breath of life into us, and that should not be taken for granted. We should strive to live our best life ever because Jesus came that we may have life and have life more abundantly (John 10:10). So try to live your best life and try not to let the issues of life weigh you down. An abundant life is a reason enough to thank him. I can't thank God enough.

I always told God that I would tell my story of how good he is to me, how he saved me, and now I am telling it. We are all on a journey, and we do not know where that journey will take us. Hopefully, we will trust the journey and trust God through the journey. God is with us always.

Did I ever stop to think why God allowed me to have these experiences? There was a well-delivered message in the question for me, and it was well-received. "Speak Lord, for your servant heareth" (1 Sam. 3:10). "Finally, let us be mindful that all scripture is given by inspiration of God and is profitable for doctrine, for reproof, for correction, for instruction in righteousness" (2 Tim. 3:16).

Search within your heart. This is a time for reflection. If you are nurturing pain, guilt, anguish, unforgiveness, etc., let them go. Allow God to purge, cleanse, and renew your heart, mind, and spirit. Sometimes our truth is ugly, and that hurts. As ugly as our truth is, that doesn't make it any less "true." That becomes our ugly truth of which we are now aware. We cannot change what happened, but we can learn from that and do better. If someone wronged us, we are to forgive him or her. If we wronged someone, we should ask him or her for forgiveness and ask God to forgive us, and we should work hard to forgive ourselves. Now go and let the healing begin. God is with you as you go forward to a better "you."

The Bride and the Bridegroom

God allowed me to foresee this event as an encouragement to the children of Evelyn Magwood:

> I was in a large warehouse, and a preparation for a wedding was taking place. I saw people gathering accessories for a wedding. The main color was gold. There was a lot of joy and jubilation as they were preparing to walk into the ceremony. I said to myself, "Why am I here?" Then the scene changed to me sitting on a large bus, looking out the window at the wedding about to take place on the beach. The bride was in an all-white wedding gown with a beaded headband of white lace for the veil. The veil came down low on the dress. I could not see the groom, but both were standing at an altar. Behind the bride, I could see an open grave. The bus driver began to drive toward the bride. He pulled over and told me to get off and that I could not go. Once I got off, he began to turn the bus toward the bride.

As the bus approached, I could see a glass panel window, and in the window were faces of women and about two men. They were smiling with joy as if welcoming the new arrival. I could feel the warmth and the love. There was no fear. (Veronica Magwood)

Let us be glad and rejoice, and give honour to him: for the marriage of the Lamb is come, and his wife hath made herself ready…and to her was granted that she should be arrayed in fine linen, clean and white: for the fine linen is the righteousness of saints… (Revelation 19:7–8).

The Gift of Love

Mama, QueenBee, Auntie Evelyn, and Lena—a mother, a grandmother, a friend, a confidant, and a spiritual advisor. A virtuous woman, one of valor ingrained with strength, patience, peace, loving-kindness, and too many positive attributes to name. A woman of integrity, dignity, and great pride, selfless in everything she did. She was "love," she lived "love," and she taught "love."

The community mother—it was not uncommon to see Mom playing with the community children: dodgeball, softball, jump rope, hopscotch, jackstones, and any kind of card games; anyone who grew up in that childhood era should remember those days very well. She would rather do things with us to keep us entertained and out of the streets safe, unbeknownst to us, from the dangers that lurked outside. The Trick or Treater Protector—yes, she accompanied the community children during those many Halloween nights to keep us safe. She was a "people's person" who gave tirelessly of herself.

Mom was the pillar of strength for our community. We had a revolving door, welcoming anyone and everyone who chose to walk in. "Auntie Evelyn, would you bake me some biscuits?" "Lena, would you make me a sweet potato pie?" "Auntie Evelyn, can I lick the bowl from the corn bread mix." Sonn, commonly called Lily Mae only by Mom, would ask, "Mrs. Magwood, would you bake a carrot cake for the church?" She met any food requests with sincerity and with a smile, for she loved to cook.

From a child's mindset, I often watched Mom asking God, how could she feed all these people? Where would the food come from? There were ten children, and Mom was the only provider and—that much I understood. Then I didn't know the story about how Jesus fed five thousand with two fish and five loaves of bread. In essence, Mom took a little and made a lot, and everyone ate and was filled. We never had much, but that which we had was rich in our spirit, for we had "her," we had each other, and we had *love*.

Maybe that is why Della would say, "As a teenager, I always loved coming over to y'all house because y'all house was always full of so much love, and I loved being around love."

I can hear Rosa Mungin say, "Lena, you have always been like a mother to me," as she told Mom how much she loved her. Doris talked about the many family reunions with Mom actively engaged in sports with the community children.

"Ahhh, those were fun days," she said. "I remember, Mama."

God gave us the gift that keeps on giving, salvation, joy, peace, strength, hope, courage, faith, forgiveness, and love; he gave us *Jesus*, and he gave us *Mom*—a sterling example of love. Thank you, Lord!

As Mom's health began to fail, I am assured that we were not preparing for her death, but we were preparing for her eternal life with our Lord and Savior Jesus Christ. That dash between her birth and eternal life years speaks for itself. The legacy she leaves will live on and be foretold for generations to come. The last of the siblings, a generation removed from this earthly realm but never from our hearts. One remembers not how the race began but how the race ended. Family, we finished strong. It takes a village to raise a child. It takes a community to care for the elderly, so I say thank you. Daisy, thank you. Mildred, thank you. Bobbi, thank you. Evelyn, thank you. Ethel, thank you. Mary, thank you. Tony, thank you. Ellen, thank you. Thelma, thank you. The word states let not thy left hand know what thy right hand doeth.

A special thank-you goes out to Gene. On December 2010, when asked why he takes such good care of Mom, Gene said, "Many years ago, Mom would cook for him, and he would always leave with $10, $20, $30, and whatever Mom could help him with. Mom never told us about their talks and that money was not worth much today, but back then, when you had nothing, something was always better."

Gene continued, "Magwood took care of me, and I'm going to take care of her."

Thank you, Lord, and thank you, Gene. Thanks to everyone within the church and community who helped from the kindness of your hearts to make Mom's transition comfortable and peaceful. Thank you, my email prayer warriors, and all others, for your many words of encouragement, prayers, and support for Mom and the family.

We are a "new" generation of the family. Auntie Rosalie, stand up for the generation before us and let the legacy of our mothers and fathers live on for generations to come. Family, let us give Auntie Rosalie our new matriarch of the family, and each other our flowers *now* so we can build memories to reflect on. Give flowers in expressions of love, support, unity, patience, and forgiveness. Give now while she can see it, smell it, and cherish it.

Mom was the last of her siblings, a generation removed. You have taken your rightful place, my queen. You have put on your long white robe, and you are walking around heaven all day, for I can imagine Jesus saying, "Welcome, thy good and faithful servant, well done! You can come on in. You can come on in."

About the Author

Photo taken by Sancha "Sheri" McBurnie

When Sandra Magwood (Hayes) was a little girl, her belief was that she would be all right regardless of what challenge may come in her life. She had not received God in her heart yet, but she had a belief within that all would be well. Although she could not explain that strong belief, she just knew and lived life without concern.

She fueled positivity and refused to allow negativity to take root in her heart and in her spirit. She watched her mom as she went through her struggles and pulled from that strength. She realized that God's prodding of her heart was leading her to stand strong through her valleys. As a result, she is strong, courageous, and relish each moment where she can encourage, motivate, and inspire others; for that brings her great joy.

Her motivating, inspiring, and encouraging stories of her obedience to God's voice are testimonials to how God kept her from death, hurt, or harm. Through her struggles, she gained strength, her spiritual growth got stronger, and she developed a personal relationship with God. Her powerful testimonials encouraged the hearts of those with challenges or those struggling with sicknesses or diagnosed diseases.

She chose to come humbly to God, knowing that his words are true. She came boldly with expectations of what God can and will do in her life. She comes with a receptive heart to embrace her journey of truth about God in her life. Dr. Sandra Hayes resides in Alexandria, Virginia.

Printed in the USA
CPSIA information can be obtained
at www.ICGtesting.com
CBHW030317231023
1444CB00002BA/7